SQUARE
PEG

CONTRIBUTORS

Robert Branson, PhD
Emeritus Professor of Old Testament
Olivet Nazarene University
Bourbonnais, Illinois

Fred Cawthorne, PhD
Associate Professor of Physics
Trevecca Nazarene University
Nashville

Vicki Copp, MDiv
Associate Pastor
Overland Park Church of the Nazarene
Overland Park, Kansas

Floyd T. Cunningham, PhD
President; Professor of the History of
Christianity
Asia-Pacific Nazarene Theological Seminary
Taytay, Philippines

H. Ray Dunning, PhD
Professor Emeritus of Theology and Philosophy
Trevecca Nazarene University
Nashville

Joel B. Green, PhD
Professor of New Testament Interpretation and
Associate Dean for the Center for Advanced
Theological Studies
Fuller Theological Seminary
Pasadena, California

Dwight Gunter, DMin
Senior Minister
Trevecca Community Church of the Nazarene
Nashville

Nina Gunter, DD
General Superintendent Emeritus
Church of the Nazarene

Philip Hamner, MDiv
Senior Pastor
Overland Park Church of the Nazarene
Overland Park, Kansas

Clair MacMillan, DD
Administrator, Canada Region, and District
Superintendent, Canada Atlantic District
Church of the Nazarene

M. Robert Mulholland Jr., PhD
Emeritus Professor of New Testament
Asbury Theological Seminary
Wilmore, Kentucky

Rick Power, MA
Senior Pastor
Olathe College Church of the Nazarene
Olathe, Kansas

Jeren Rowell, EdD
District Superintendent, Kansas City District
Church of the Nazarene

Mary Lou Shea, ThD
Associate Professor of Christian History and
Mission
Eastern Nazarene College
Quincy, Massachusetts

Bethany Hull Somers, MDiv
Senior Minister
Mount Vernon Church of the Nazarene
Mount Vernon, Washington

Carla Sunberg, MA
Evangelism Pastor
Grace Point Church of the Nazarene
Fort Wayne, Indiana

Al Truesdale, PhD
Emeritus Professor of Philosophy of Religion
and Christian Ethics
Nazarene Theological Seminary
Kansas City

SQUARE
PEG

Why Wesleyans
Aren't Fundamentalists

AL TRUESDALE

editor

BEACON HILL PRESS
OF KANSAS CITY

Copyright 2012 by Beacon Hill Press of Kansas City

ISBN 978-0-8341-2793-7

Cover Design: Arthur Cherry
Interior Design: Sharon Page

Library of Congress Cataloging-in-Publication Data

Square peg : why Wesleyans aren't fundamentalist / Al Truesdale, editor.
    p. cm.
  Includes bibliographical references.
  ISBN 978-0-8341-2793-7 (pbk.)
  1. Wesleyan Church—Doctrines. 2. Fundamentalism. I. Truesdale, Albert, 1941-
  BX9995.W45S68 2012
  230'.7—dc23

                                        2011042140

10 9 8 7 6 5 4 3 2 1

CONTENTS

INTRODUCTION

At a time when parts of some Christian denominations are abandoning doctrines essential to the Christian faith, we should praise God for all in Christ's church who remain zealous for the faith "once delivered unto the saints" (Jude v. 3, KJV). We grieve when controlling voices in some denominations reveal that their primary allegiance is to the intellectual norms of the eighteenth-century Enlightenment, moral relativism, and religious pluralism, and so deny Jesus Christ to be the world's Redeemer. In contrast, we rejoice over those who continue to champion the primacy of the Scriptures in all matters pertaining to faith and practice and who with conviction embrace the historic Christian creeds—Nicene, Chalcedonian, and Apostles'. Such shared convictions that unite orthodox Christians are far more important than things about which we disagree. John Wesley said all faithful Christians share "the same Captain of . . . salvation," are "companion[s] in the kingdom," and are "joint-heir[s] of [Christ's] glory."[1] He described this as the "catholic spirit."[2]

Without becoming divisive or claiming perfection in Christian doctrine, the various denominations hold theological positions that reflect their Christian experience, history, and understanding of the Scriptures. For example, Presbyterians reject the role of bishops, while Episcopalians and United Methodists endorse it. There are historical as well as biblical reasons for both positions. Calvinists and Lutherans don't quite agree about the meaning of the Lord's Supper. Wesleyans and Calvinists disagree about what "election" means. And Lutherans and Baptists are far apart on infant baptism.

One day the Lord will perfect his church, and then what all of us know in part will be known in full (see 1 Cor. 13:9-13). Until then, let us never cease to give thanks for faithful sisters and brothers and never cease remembering them in our prayers (see Eph. 1:15-16).

In this book we will examine two significantly different ways of understanding the nature and role of the Bible that mark different parts of Christ's church. The first is represented by fundamentalism;[3] the second by Wesleyan theology. Differences reach even further, to the nature of revelation, the role of the Holy Spirit, the way Christians should appraise the natural sciences, and even the nature of Christian discipleship.

The goal is to help persons in Wesleyan denominations, such as the Free Methodist Church, the Wesleyan Church, and the Church of the Nazarene, clearly understand how Wesleyan theology distinctively and richly addresses some of the topics that identify fundamentalism. We shall see that differences between fundamentalism and Wesleyan theology are so important that denominations in the Wesleyan tradition cannot adopt fundamentalism without forfeiting essential parts of what it means to be Wesleyan.

While we believe that in major ways Wesleyan theology transcends fundamentalism, we recognize that Wesleyans and their sisters and brothers who are fundamentalists share a love for Jesus Christ and his inaugurated kingdom. Let Wesley's words to a Catholic Christian characterize our disposition toward one another: "So far as we can, let us always rejoice to strengthen each other's hands in God. Above all, let us . . . take heed . . . [not to] fall . . . short of the religion of love."[4]

The structural plan for this book is as follows. Chapter 1 provides an overview of the history of fundamentalism and, to some extent, describes its impact on denominations in the Wesleyan tradition. Chapter 2 examines differences between a fundamentalist and a Wesleyan doctrine of the Scriptures. Because of fundamentalism's doctrine of Scripture, fundamentalists read the creation accounts in Genesis quite differently from Wesleyans. Consequently, chapter 3 contrasts how people in biblical times viewed the world against how moderns view the cosmos. In chapter 4 we compare and contrast fundamentalist theology and Wesleyan theology. The fifth chapter observes how fundamentalism erred, even if unintentionally, in its response to modernity. Building upon that discussion, in chapter 6, a representative of the natural sciences will explore the relationship between modern science and the Christian faith. The chapter will show that Wesleyan theology has no interest in pitting legitimate science against orthodox faith. Chapter 7 discusses a Wesleyan understanding of unity-in-diversity, or a catholic spirit. Finally, chapter 8 examines the relationship between biblical authority and Christian holiness in the Wesleyan tradition.

This book contains historical, biblical, scientific, and theological exposition. Its goal is to be both informative and formative. With the exception of chapter 1, following each chapter is a practical discussion of why that chapter matters. Most of these follow-up pieces emerged from discussions among groups of laypersons led by clergy. Some of them are written by clergy as practical pastoral counsel.

The times call for Christians who will embrace apostolic Christian faith with informed conviction. From its beginning, the Wesleyan tradition has sought to be holistically informed by Scripture (principally), Christian tradition, reason, and experience. It has advocated a religion of the heart that entails the Holy Spirit renewing the whole person, in community, after the image of Christ in righteousness and true holiness. For Wesleyans, the proof of the gospel resides primarily in its being lived, in transformed life, not in logic and argumentation.

John Wesley was deeply committed to informed and thoughtful discipleship. To educate the Methodists he produced a thirty-volume library meant to foster thoughtful and well-informed piety. In 1748

Wesley created Kingswood School near Bristol to educate children of coal miners. He placed Hebrew and Greek grammar in the curriculum so children could learn to read the Bible in its original languages. And when Wesley studied and sought to explain the Scriptures, he drew upon the best scholarly tools available. "Faith seeking understanding"[5] guided Wesley's own life and his aspirations for the Methodists.

The point of all this is that the Wesleyan tradition offers no haven for any form of Christianity that shrinks from honest and rigorous consideration of all aspects of the Christian faith and its relationship to the world. Wesleyans have characteristically shied away from marrying the Christian faith to a worldview in one era that might leave it a widow in the next. A thoughtful embrace of apostolic Christian faith is its aspiration. Denominations that stand in the Wesleyan tradition are at their best when they advocate a vital faith that seeks understanding through a bold examination of the results of all human exploration, whether in technology, in the sciences, or through historical research.

In that spirit our study will proceed.

A HISTORICAL OVERVIEW OF
FUNDAMENTALISM

Floyd T. Cunningham, PhD

■ In the United States and Great Britain a fundamentalist response to perceived threats to orthodox Christian doctrine occurred in the latter part of the nineteenth and early part of the twentieth centuries. It was a reaction to something broadly known as theological modernism. Fundamentalists thought that modernism surrendered historic and essential Christian doctrines. Later, in the twentieth century, fundamentalism also confronted the challenge of secular humanism infiltrating the church and society.

In this chapter we will briefly profile fundamentalism in its American and, to some extent, British forms. This profile will provide a basis for the chapters that follow.

What Is Fundamentalism?

Scholars are reluctant to offer simple definitions of fundamentalism. The movement is too diverse for that. Only informally organized, the different components of fundamentalism share a common history and set of characteristics. Biblical scholar James Barr uses over three hundred pages to "define" fundamentalism. Nevertheless, he initially identifies three of the movement's most pronounced traits: (1) a very strong emphasis on the inerrancy of the Bible, the absence from it of any error; (2) a strong hostility to modern critical study of the Bible; and (3) an assurance that those who do not share the fundamentalists' religious viewpoint are not really "true Christians."[1] Nancy T. Ammerman discusses three deciding characteristics of fundamentalism: (1) evangelism (a kinship shared with evangelicals); (2) inerrancy of the Bible, meaning that it is free of all error of fact or principle (providing "an accurate description of science and history, as well as morality and religion"); and (3) premillennialism (true of most fundamentalists).[2] Historian George M. Marsden tentatively defines a fundamentalist as "an evangelical who is militant in opposition to liberal theology in the churches or to changes in our cultural values or mores, such as those associated with 'secular humanism.'"[3] Marsden also observes that fundamentalism is a "distinct version of evangelical Christianity uniquely shaped by the circumstances of America in the early twentieth century"; fundamentalists found "themselves living in a culture that by the 1920s was openly turning away from God."[4]

The term "fundamentalism" was coined in 1920 and derived from a series of booklets titled *The Fundamentals*. They were published in the United States between 1910 and 1915 (discussed below). The booklets used the term "fundamentals" to identify doctrines thought to be essential and nonnegotiable for orthodox Christian faith.

To preserve what it believes to be orthodox Christian theology, fundamentalism champions a view of biblical authority that emphasizes the Bible's inerrancy in matters of science and history, as well as faith and practice. Its proponents believe much of modern biblical scholarship has resulted in undercutting the Bible's authority and reducing it to a narrow historical and cultural context. This, fundamentalists believe, has fostered unbelief and moral relativity. By contrast, the Bible as written and received presents the worldview to which orthodox Christians should conform. Consequently, the Bible must not be subjected to literary and historical analysis as are other ancient documents.

Doing so only undermines the Bible as the revealed, inerrant, and authoritative Word of God. Against all perceived opponents of the Bible and Christian doctrine, fundamentalists uphold the literal meaning of Scripture. Consequently, they reject the modern theories of evolution and uphold creationism as they think Genesis teaches it.

Given what late nineteenth-century fundamentalists saw as the moral and religious disintegration of Western society, it is not surprising that they thought of Christ's return and the end times in that light. And given the unchanging character of the Bible as fundamentalists understood it, it is to be expected that they reacted negatively to some earthshaking movements such as the rise of feminism, which, they thought, jeopardized the God-given hierarchy of familial authority as taught in the Bible.

The Wesleyan response to fundamentalism was mixed, but ultimately Wesleyans recognized important differences between themselves and fundamentalists. What was of more concern to Wesleyans than defending a particular view of biblical inspiration was presenting what the Bible teaches about Christ's sanctifying work.

The Nineteenth-Century Antecedents of Fundamentalism

Influenced greatly by the holiness revivals of the mid-nineteenth century, Protestants such as Dwight L. Moody rallied around an emphasis upon regeneration and a life of Christian piety. Fundamentalism represented a narrowing of this broad nineteenth-century evangelical tradition.

Let's discuss three nineteenth-century antecedents of twentieth-century fundamentalism.

1. In the 1890s, in America and Great Britain, many evangelicals who promoted revivalism organized prophecy conferences, the most prominent of which was the Niagara Bible Conference. With the exception of 1884, the Niagara Bible Conference met annually from 1876 to 1897. In 1883 it met in Niagara-on-the-Lake, Ontario,

Canada, the place that gave the conference its name. The conferences built upon the assumption that recent and future events in human history were foretold in the Bible in coded form. In the prophecy conferences, nineteenth-century fundamentalism achieved its characteristic form.

A perspective known as dispensationalism became a prominent explanation of what the Bible foretells. Dispensationalism is rooted in the teaching of John Nelson Darby (1800-1882), a founder of the Plymouth Brethren in Ireland and England. It is the belief that God chronologically acts in history according to distinct dispensations or periods of revelation and divine purpose. Each dispensation is marked by a fitting covenant and has its own divine goal and revelatory content. There is no uniform agreement among dispensationalists on the number or content of the dispensations.

Dispensationalism is associated with millennialism. Millennialism is the belief that Christ will reign upon the earth for one thousand years prior to the consummation of the kingdom of God and the final judgment. Millennialism rests upon Rev. 20:1-6, which speaks of the Devil being bound for one thousand years. During that time the Devil would not be able to deceive the nations. The holy martyrs would come to life and reign with Christ during the millennium (vv. 4-5). After that, the Devil would be "let out for a little while" (v. 3). There was a division of opinion among millennialists over whether Christ would return before the millennium and establish his reign or whether the kingdom of God, with Christ reigning spiritually, would progressively advance on earth until the millennium of peace would dawn, after which Christ would return. Those who held to the first interpretation were known as premillennialists. Those holding the second position were postmillennialists.

The prophecy conferences supported premillennial dispensationalism. Dispensationalists reasoned that Christ was not about to build his kingdom on earth by using human hands. So they embraced a premillennialist interpretation of Scripture. They harbored pessimistic expectations for the redemption of society and considered technological advances and social improvements to be insignificant in God's design. For them, world history confirmed that things would get worse, not better, before Christ's return. Any sign of the world's decline was looked upon eagerly as a sign of Christ's soon return.[5]

By contrast, the perfectionist ideals of the nineteenth-century Holiness Movement and postmillennialism influenced social thought from a different direction. They promoted optimistic expectations for human progress in history. It seemed to them that God was working out his will on earth, even as it was done in heaven. God was actively eradicating evil here below and building his kingdom. The side of Darwinism that suggested the evolution of humankind was from lower to higher life-forms confirmed their optimism. Postmillennialists, as they were known, rejoiced in many of the advances in industry, technology, and social progress. They saw human enterprise and reason as the means by which God was completing his kingdom. Thus many of the perfectionists who embraced the promise of Christian holiness welcomed science and history as part of humankind's great upward march.

Others equally committed to holiness held an amillennialist position. They taught that the thousand-year reign is figurative rather than literal and refers to eternity. In their reading of the Bible there was no time, place, or reason for a kingdom of God on earth either preceding or following Christ's second coming.

2. A second major factor in the development of fundamentalism was a type of theology known as Princeton theology. It came from Princeton Theological Seminary. The Princeton theologians, discussed in chapter 5, stood at a critical distance from much of what characterized fundamentalism. They were indebted to the teachings of John Calvin and Scottish common-sense realism. The latter taught that nature as immediately and plainly perceived conveys certain truths about itself and about God as Creator. Princeton theologians such as Charles Hodge

accepted the "givenness" or plain, "common-sense" meaning of texts such as the Bible. Historical criticism, which looked beyond plain meanings to the historical context of the text, influenced other seminaries in the late nineteenth century, but not Princeton. Its teachers presented a defense of what they considered Scripture's plain meaning and what they believed to be an accurate presentation of Calvinist theology.[6]

3. A third major factor was the challenge presented by geological and biological inquiries into the origins of the world and humankind. Darwin's 1859 *On the Origin of Species* raised the question of how literally the Bible's account of creation could be taken. Darwin's research seemed to confirm the theories of many leading American scientists who had concluded from geological evidence that the world was much older than a literal reading of the Bible indicated. At first, few clergy reacted negatively against the theory of evolution. Many theologians, including Methodists Thomas Ralston, John Miley, and Olin Curtis, were able to harmonize an ancient earth and a non-atheistic theory of evolution with Genesis and Christian principles. Other biblical scholars suggested that on such matters as the computation of dates and simple chronology biblical writers sometimes contradicted each other and were sometimes mistaken on matters of historical fact. They accepted that Hebrew writers might have adapted some of their literature from other cultures. But on matters of faith and practice, the Bible remained authoritative; it was God's faithful Word to men and women. The overriding interest was the conversion of men and women to Christ. They hoped soon to evangelize the entire world. Preaching the gospel overrode lesser interests.

Many nineteenth-century evangelicals interpreted the Bible in a way that emphasized the Scripture's intention to speak authoritatively only on matters of faith and practice. They normally left science and history free to pursue their own goals. Because God is Truth, scientific and historic inquiries could only succeed in magnifying God's glory. These evangelicals sought to unify religion and science. When, for example, Genesis says the world was created in six days, and Darwinists say it took several million years; many evangelicals resolved the apparent conflict by interpreting "day" (*yom*, Hebrew) as meaning an indeterminate period of time. They interpreted the remnants of animal instinct in men and women as pointing to the carnal nature about which Paul spoke. The "animal" remnants are at war with the higher, spiritual nature of God's image in humankind. Evangelicals who interpreted Genesis in this way thought that God had at some time conferred a soul upon primal beings. Through the soul, God created Adam and Eve as human beings. Evangelicals who followed this path looked to prehistory for a threshold when self-consciousness and conscience developed. They worked to harmonize science and religion.[7]

While some evangelicals could achieve reconciliation between Darwin and Genesis, others could not. Indebted to Francis Bacon and common-sense realism, Charles Hodge accepted as truth about the world only what was immediately apparent and in line with common sense. There is no immediate evidence that change of the Darwinian magnitude has occurred among plants or animals. Nature proceeds according to immutable laws that common sense can discover and confirm.

Hodge was convinced that not only is God unchanging but so also is the natural order in its essential form; it is as God created it, not as it allegedly evolved. Though Hodge did not oppose science or reason, he was distrustful of speculative theory of the kind he believed Darwin practiced. Hypotheses such as evolution were based on unfounded and subjective interpretations of data. Human reason exercised as Darwin had employed it is too tainted by original sin to be trusted. He crafted a doctrine of inspiration that defended biblical inerrancy in all these matters.

Hodge was also suspicious of evangelist Charles G. Finney's "new methods" for revivals and his promotion of the causes of women and the abolition of slaves. Both of these emphases departed from the literal and plain teaching of the inspired Scriptures, as Hodge understood it. Unlike Hodge, Finney relied upon a dynamic understanding of biblical authority, attributed to the Holy Spirit, instead of relying upon the inspired text alone.[8]

The Early Twentieth Century

In the early decades of the twentieth century, certain evangelicals sensed deeply that modernist trends in their denominations threatened the faith. Some of these persons had been influenced by the late nineteenth-century prophecy conferences, and others by the kind of Calvinist theology Benjamin Warfield was teaching at Princeton. Although Warfield, in particular, was untroubled by the thought of humankind's evolution, he and others thought the inerrancy of the Bible was under attack from scholars who used the methods of historical criticism (analyzing the books of the Bible primarily as historical and literary documents, not primarily as bearers of revelation).[9] Related to this issue during these years were several significant matters.

1. Modernism (position that Christian beliefs must be restated in ways that comply with modern forms of understanding): enemy of the faith. Like their nineteenth-century forebears, these fundamentalists believed the plain and literal meanings of the Bible must be preserved. They were determined to safeguard its inspiration and authority and attacked modernists for rejecting the Bible's plain meanings. Those whom they called modernists found clues to the authorship of biblical texts, their period of composition, and their place of origin by using historical and literary methods. For instance, their research led them to believe that the first five books of the Bible (the Pentateuch), traditionally attributed to Moses, were in fact drawn from a variety of sources at different times and that close attention to the text confirms this. They thought the Pentateuch also contains contrasting theological emphases. All this unnerved many Christians and invited opposition from fundamentalists.

From the modernist perspective, if we expect contemporary persons to receive the Bible's truth, its historical roots must be taken seriously. The Bible's truth lies beneath legends and allusions woven into the biblical narrative. For modernists, close observation and examination are the criteria of authority. They could appreciate subjectively the beneficial value of biblical religion without having to accept its worldview—its claims about God and the world. Moreover, for them modern thought is more than a tool of theology; it is the final standard for religious belief. Modernists generally rejected Christ's virgin birth, deity, and resurrection in their efforts to "save" Christianity from being rejected by moderns as superstitious and unworthy of trust. They wanted to establish an intellectually acceptable way to understand the Bible and its message. For modernists, Jesus was thought to be as nearly godlike as any person might be. He was an eternal example of the religious and moral perfection for which humans long. This was modernist "gospel." Baptist Harry E. Fosdick maintained that the historical method would save the church from intellectual adolescence. He insisted that what is vital to Christianity is the "personal experience of God in Christ."[10] The heart of religion is the intuitive feelings of human beings. At the same time, religion can be adequately understood on the basis of reason alone. A proper relationship to God requires religious creativity and an expanded understanding on our part.[11]

Fundamentalists rejected modernism and refused to let the Bible be analyzed as secular documents might be. Rather, it is the Word of God and results from divine authorship. Accepting the Bible's supernatural origin is a matter of Christian faith. The Bible cannot be analyzed historically lest its divine origin and inspiration be called into question. Furthermore, men and women will never be saved if they doubt either the divine origin of the Bible or any of its teachings. Fundamentalists were certain other Christians were succumbing to the spirit of the age by accepting the conclusions of historical research—the historical method—when applied to the Bible.

Characteristically, fundamentalism was neither irrational nor theologically untutored. The fundamentalist goal was to save Christianity from rationalism and humanism and thus to preserve both the Bible's sacredness and the deity of Christ. Saving "orthodox" Christianity was the mission. Though some fundamentalists regarded scholarship with suspicion, most of their dissatisfaction was aimed at what they judged as false pretenses to scholarship. In the name of scholarship, many universities spewed out the "putridness of infidelity upon humanity."[12]

2. *The Fundamentals.* As mentioned early in this chapter, *The Fundamentals*, a paperback twelve-volume series (published between 1910 and 1915) written by numerous American and British scholars and ministers, identified the essential Christian doctrines. They were published as *The Fundamentals: A Testimony to the Truth.* The volumes were widely distributed—as many as three million copies. Fundamental doctrines were also in evidence in the fourteen-point creed of the 1878 Niagara Bible Conference and the 1910 five-point statement of the Presbyterian General Assembly. Fundamentalists have never uniformly agreed on the precise number and identity of the fundamentals.

The fundamental doctrines, or beliefs, as stated in *The Fundamentals* are as follows:

1. The inerrancy and verbal inspiration of Scripture
2. The Trinity
3. The virgin birth and incarnation of Christ
4. Original sin
5. The atonement of Christ
6. The resurrection of Christ
7. A premillennial return of Christ
8. Spiritual rebirth
9. Bodily resurrection and eternal salvation or damnation

The Fundamentals also attacked evolution and the social gospel. To these nine fundamentals were added a defense of a literal reading of the Genesis account of creation.

3. In defense of formalism. Faith in progress waned as the Great War engulfed and destroyed Germany, once considered by many the finest Christian society. Not only had Germany been the author of the Great War, but, American Protestants remembered, its biblical scholars had also been the first to doubt the Bible's inerrancy. Many Americans linked German wartime atrocities to this kind of German scholarship. They believed the trail of German criticism led not only to challenging the inerrancy of the Scriptures but to eliminating all moral absolutes as well. To them, the historical method implied that what people believe to be true emerged and changed through time. Thus religious belief and morality were relative. This rejection of absolute truth was part of a broader revolt against formalism, a revolt fundamentalists opposed.

Formalism is the belief that laws are universal and unchanging, that they transcend and govern the physical and moral world. The revolt against formalism held that laws are not universal and timeless. Instead, they are limited, useful tools for certain situations and periods. Fundamentalists saw this revolt as a rejection of standards by which morality and any other worthwhile aspect of culture can be established. Moral laws, fundamentalists insisted, are directly attributable to unchanging biblical principles. Neither the Bible nor morals are historically relative.

Fundamentalists needed a religion that remains the same while the rest of life is rapidly changing. They established and attended churches that supported such sure foundations. And they focused their attention on forces that threatened religious and moral structures. Increasingly, they saw themselves as entrusted by God to defend the true biblical faith besieged by modernism and Darwinist science.

In the Bible fundamentalists found a sure foundation that could withstand the corrosive influences of modern unbelief and Darwinism. The biblical story of creation established human uniqueness as having been given in a moment of creation. Humans were created in God's image. Adam's fall explained the appearance of sin, guilt, and the failures of the race. Darwinist theory, by contrast, debased human life as fundamentalists believed the Bible presented it. By implication Darwinism eliminated any plan for creation and redemption authored and superintended by God.[13]

4. Emergence of the evangelicals. The famous trial of John Scopes in 1925 in Dayton, Tennessee, for allegedly teaching evolution in public schools contrary to state law was a legal victory for fundamentalism. William Jennings Bryan defended the state and what was in essence the fundamentalist position on creation. Clarence Darrow, who defended Scopes, ridiculed Bryan's deficient knowledge of modern science and the Bible. Bryan won the battle, but many believed he and the fundamentalists lost the war.[14]

But fundamentalism was not driven from the field at Dayton. For a time, it lost momentum, but quickly revived. Local fundamentalist congregations experienced a few major setbacks. Attempts to assure a fundamentalist orientation for the major denominations failed. But nondenominational organizations, schools such as Dallas Theological Seminary and Wheaton College, radio broadcasts, and periodicals flourished. The *Scofield* annotated edition of the King James Version, published in 1909 by Cyrus Scofield, which linked verses together to substantiate premillennialism, remained popular. Many independent Bible schools were established. Representing the premillennialist side of fundamentalism, the Moody Bible Institute became closely identified with fundamentalism. Its president, James Gray, believed fundamentalism would bring revival to the United States.[15]

Meanwhile, at Princeton, theologian J. Gresham Machen attempted unsuccessfully to keep the seminary true to a strict interpretation of the Calvinist Westminster Confession of Faith—the 1646 doctrinal standard of Presbyterians. But he and other conservative Presbyterians could not prevent the direction their denomination was taking. Finally, in 1929, Machen, along with three other Princeton professors, formed Westminster Theological Seminary. In 1936 he founded a separate denomination (later called the Orthodox Presbyterian Church).[16]

During the 1930s, fundamentalists rallied around nondenominational organizations, such as Moody and Bob Jones University, and local leaders, such as William Bell Riley in Minnesota. Some became reactionary in politics. Fundamentalists were all but forgotten in the nationwide publicity favoring the denominations affiliated with the Federation of Christian Churches, which had been formed in 1908. Regulatory agencies even denied to fundamentalists the possibility of broadcasting on the radio. A darker side of fundamentalism showed itself in the 1930s when some leaders sympathized with Fascism and anti-Semitism.[17]

Fundamentalists led by Carl McIntire organized the American Council of Christian Churches in 1941. Not all fundamentalists followed. Fundamentalism divided between evangelicals (the self-designation of those who were open to certain literary and historical approaches to the Scriptures) and fundamentalists.[18] Evangelicals welcomed Billy Graham's campaigns, which brought together many varieties of Protestants, while fundamentalists argued for a separation from the world and so-called Christians in denominations that, by fundamentalist standards, rejected the orthodox faith. Fundamentalists adhered to the King James Version of the Bible and attributed a high level of inspiration to it.[19] Evangelicals saw the need for newer translations. They also sought to come to terms with the mounting evidence for evolution. In 1942 evangelicals under Harold John Ockenga organized the National Association of Evangelicals. The NAE and McIntire's organization intended to counteract the Federal Council of Churches and its successor, the National Council of Churches, which was organized in 1950.[20]

In the 1950s both fundamentalists and evangelicals were driven back toward the cultural center by the country's spirit of patriotism against "atheistic communism."

23

Conclusion

Denominations whose theological identity is rooted in the Wesleyan tradition, including those shaped by the nineteenth-century Holiness Movement, have given mixed responses to and appraisals of fundamentalism. Wesleyans have found it difficult to embrace fundamentalism for numerous reasons.

First, historically fundamentalism has been articulated within a predominantly Calvinist theological structure. Wesleyans have assigned prominence to the doctrine of Christian holiness in a way not normally supported by Calvinist theology. Wesleyans also have a significantly different understanding of the scope of Christ's atonement—rejecting the doctrine of predestination—and the conditions for continuing in the Christian life. The gulf between Wesleyanism and fundamentalism became more apparent when J. Gresham Machen and others defined fundamentalism strictly in the language of the Westminster Confession and strict Calvinism.

Second, Wesleyans will not commit to a single understanding of eschatology. There are two reasons for this: (1) they do not believe the New Testament treats eschatology in neat and narrow formulas, and (2) they do not believe questions about the end times are of essential theological importance. What one believes about the end times is unworthy of divisive argument. Wesleyans are far more interested in holy living than in charting God's future. They believe the most important protection against heresy is not right argument but the purity and power that proceeds from the Holy Spirit.

Third, Wesleyans simply cannot embrace fundamentalism's doctrine of the Scriptures. As subsequent chapters will show, Wesleyans are thoroughly committed to the primacy and authority of the Scriptures in all matters pertaining to doctrine and Christian practice. But for reasons that rest upon what they think constitutes the Bible's authority,

Wesleyans cannot embrace a fundamentalist doctrine of biblical inerrancy.[21]

As will be seen in chapter 5, Wesleyans are much more in line with Martin Luther and John Calvin than are fundamentalists. The most insightful and influential theologians of the Church of the Nazarene, for example, have repeatedly shown the disjunction between the two appraisals of the Bible's authority. Theologian H. Orton Wiley rejected the fundamentalists' "mechanical" view of Scripture because it excluded the role of human reason and any serious consideration of the social and historical contexts of the authors.[22] Ralph Earle, longtime New Testament professor at Nazarene Theological Seminary in Kansas City, urged the denomination to understand that its doctrine of biblical inspiration derived from John Wesley and from roots deep in the Church of England (e.g., Richard Hooker [1554–1600]).[23] Accordingly, he explained that unlike fundamentalists, Nazarenes should understand that plenary, or full, inspiration applies to the Scriptures as a whole. The Bible, Earle taught, is "infallible" in what it intends to convey: truth concerning God and salvation.[24] He also was among the team of translators for the *New International Version* of the Bible. Theologian W. T. Purkiser said the Nazarene Article of Faith on Scripture saved the denomination from "bondage to a fundamentalist literalism which affirms the dictation of each word of the original autographs, and which sometimes seems to extend the same sanctity to a certain English version."[25] In harmony with John Wesley, these and more recent Nazarene theologians stressed the primary role of the Holy Spirit in the hearts and lives of the Bible's hearers. They have pointed out that inspiration resides with the Holy Spirit and is not the independent property of the Bible. Only the Holy Spirit can make the Bible's message of salvation a living and transforming word from God.[26]

Fourth, because of its doctrine of Scripture, Wesleyans cannot support the negative appraisal of modern biological and geological science that characterizes fundamentalism. H. Orton Wiley was typical of a Wesleyan refusal to use the book of Genesis for imposing limitations on what modern science can teach us about origins. Wiley said the poetic "creation hymn" of Gen. 1–3 answers the question of *who* God is, not how or when God created the universe.[27] As early as 1960, the denomination's theological textbook, *Exploring Our Christian Faith*, stated that any attempt to read modern science into the Genesis account of creation inflicts an "injustice [on] both Genesis and science."[28]

THE WESLEYAN DOCTRINE OF
SCRIPTURE
(As Contrasted with Fundamentalism)
M. Robert Mulholland Jr., PhD

■ The doctrine of Scripture is comparable in importance to the doctrine of the Trinity in the struggles Christians have had in defining the Christian faith. With the rise of biblical criticism during the Enlightenment, the battle lines became sharply defined and, in some sense, came to a head in the fundamentalist-modernist controversies of the early twentieth century.

The Wesleyan movement, beginning with John and Charles Wesley in the eighteenth century, emerged within the larger philosophical world of the Enlightenment. Wesley, and his descendants in the Wesleyan tradition, promoted a high view of Scripture. Wesley and most of his descendants developed a doctrine of Scripture that focused on its role in transforming the believer's inner being as the ground for reordering behavior. Fundamentalism, on the other hand, developed a doctrine of Scripture that tended to focus on reordering behavior in obedience to a body of propositional truths.

Fundamentalism and the Bible

Fundamentalism's doctrine of Scripture is somewhat difficult to define, primarily because fundamentalists hold diverse understandings of Scripture. While all fundamentalists support a high view of Scripture, such topics as why Scripture is believed to be the Word of God, the meaning of inerrancy, and the nature of biblical authority are explained in different ways within fundamentalism.

One group believes Scripture was dictated by God to persons who were little more than secretaries writing down what they heard. In other words, Scripture is the words of God that lack any human influence other than the writers' handwriting. Hence, Scripture contains the "literal" words of God.

Another group of fundamentalists believes Scripture was dictated by God to persons who had some freedom to express what they heard in their own languages and personalities. This accounts for the various literary styles[1] evident in the Bible, without diminishing God's direct action. This group's doctrine of Scripture stresses the inspiration of Scripture, not its dictation.

Another difficulty in trying to define fundamentalism's doctrine of Scripture is how best to define "inerrant" and "infallible." Doing so involves two general subgroups: (1) those who acknowledge the role of textual criticism (analysis of a text's history of formation) and the variant readings in the multitude of manuscripts available today but who say that only the original autographs[2] were inerrant;[3] and (2) those who reject textual criticism altogether and teach that only translations from the Textus Receptus[4] are inerrant. A subgroup of the second position, the "King James Only Movement," thinks the creators of the King James Version were guided by God. It is the only authoritative English version of the Bible and the only version free from error.[5]

This diversity is acknowledged by some fundamentalists but is not thought to be divisive. "Fundamentalists may hold the doctrine of the verbal inspiration and inerrancy of Scripture with equal strength without sharing the same beliefs about text-critical matters and theories of translation."[6]

Underlying most, if not all, of these variant understandings of Scripture is the question of the nature of truth (also discussed in chap. 4). Generally, in fundamentalism, truth is understood propositionally: a set of divine declarations and claims about God, creation, human existence, sin, redemption, salvation, sanctification, and eternal life. Once this perception of truth is established as Scripture's underlying reality, the Bible becomes a collection of propositions that lay out the parameters or limits for understanding God, history, creation, and so on. The basic question then becomes the reliability of this body of propositions. To insure the validity and reliability of any biblical proposition, the whole Bible must be inerrant and infallible. Even though human agents were involved, their involvement must be just as inerrant and infallible as the propositions they transmitted. Otherwise, the authority of these writings would be at risk (see chap. 8 for further discussion of the nature of biblical authority).

One difficulty associated with this doctrine of Scripture involves the nature of God. To put it simply (hopefully not too simply), God becomes the creator and monitor of a set of propositional truths that are primarily legal in nature. As the formulator of these propositional truths, God, the Judge, administers justice to those who disagree with or violate the divine propositions. Failure to embrace any of the propositions means sinning against God. Consequently, redemption becomes principally legal and propositional. Christ's death is a *ransom* paid to someone. Christ is the legally acceptable, innocent *substitute* for the *penalty* sinners should have suffered; he is the legally sufficient *sacrifice* made to God. Like this one, all the Bible's propositions are rationally comprehensible explanations of what God has done and how persons "gain" and "maintain" acceptance before God. The propositions can be comprehended by anyone who thinks properly.

Another problem associated with a fundamentalist doctrine of Scripture concerns God's self-disclosure in Jesus. God became incarnate in Jesus of Nazareth, a first-century Palestinian Jew. But as the Gospels show repeatedly, many of Jesus' contemporaries did not recognize what God was doing. John explains, "He came to what was his own, and his own people did not accept him" (John 1:11). Even John the Baptist, who knew he was to be forerunner to the Messiah, asks, "Are you the one who is to come, or are we to wait for another?" (Matt. 11:3). People disagreed about who Jesus was: "Some say John the Baptist, but others Elijah, and still others Jeremiah or one of the prophets" (16:14); "And there was considerable complaining about him among the crowds. While some were saying, 'He is a good man,' others were saying, 'No, he is deceiving the crowd'" (John 7:12). Even the disciples were unclear about Jesus' identity (Mark 6:52; 9:32; Luke 9:45; John 12:16).

If the Word become flesh had such an ambiguous reception among those who should have recognized God in their midst, if God's ultimate revelation was not clearly understood by those who saw God enfleshed, obviously much more is involved in perceiving and receiving what the Scriptures reveal than merely processing rational propositions. Did not Jesus explain that very thing to Nicodemus (John 3:1-14)? And Paul made this abundantly clear to the Christians in Corinth by stressing the central and irreplaceable role of the Holy Spirit in our learning the things of God (1 Cor. 2:6-14). Should we be surprised that the revelation of God in Scripture has received such a mixed reception? It has not been received as one might receive a proposition. If the Word disclosed in human flesh was not correctly received, why should we expect the Word clothed in human words to fare any better?

When understood as a collection of propositional truths, God's revelation becomes "information." By contrast, in the words of Thomas Merton, "God manifests himself not in information but in life-giving power."[7] The living and transforming God himself, not information about him, is the *content* of revelation. Similarly, John Wesley believed Scripture to be the vehicle of a transforming encounter with God, resulting in regeneration of the inner being and the consequent reordering of one's entire life. The Wesleyan doctrine of Scripture moves in a direction quite different from that of fundamentalism.

John Wesley on Scripture

Perhaps the best starting point for understanding the Wesleyan doctrine of Scripture is with John Wesley's instructions for reading Scripture:[8]

This is the way to understand the things of God: "Meditate thereon day and night" [Josh. 1:8; Ps. 1:2];[9] so shall you attain the best knowledge, even to "know the only true God, and Jesus Christ whom he hath sent" [John 17:3]. And this knowledge will lead you "to love Him, because He hath first loved us" [1 John 4:19]; yea, "to love the Lord your God with all your heart, and with all your soul, and with all your mind, and with all your strength" [Mark 12:30]. . . . And in consequence of this, while you joyfully experience all the holy tempers described in this book, you will likewise be outwardly "holy as He that hath called you is holy, in all manner of conversation" [1 Pet. 1:15].

Wesley's doctrine of Scripture is disclosed in this passage. *First,* Scripture is the means by which we come to know God. Knowing God, however, is not simply a matter of cognitive knowledge; it necessarily involves experiential or transformational knowledge. Wesley's focus is on a vital love relationship with God, not upon propositional knowledge about God: "This knowledge will lead you 'to love Him, because He hath first loved us'; yea, 'to love the Lord your God with all your heart, and with all your soul, and with all your mind, and with all your strength.'" This is clear in Wesley's admonition to "meditate thereon day and night." It seems obvious Wesley intends that the Bible's role is to lead believers to live consistently in an ever-deepening relationship with God. This is what constant reflection upon Scripture should nurture. Wesley practiced what he taught, for his writings virtually "bleed Scripture," as do the hymns of his brother Charles. Their perceptual framework was thoroughly scriptural, and their lives witnessed to a living relationship with God.

Second, Wesley saw that as Christians' inner beings are shaped by living with the Scriptures, they will "joyfully experience all the holy tempers[10] described in this book." The consequence of this inner mode of being and the real proof of the Scriptures is a life that is "outwardly 'holy as He that hath called you is holy, in all manner of conversation.'"[11] Apart from that, for Wesley, speaking of the Bible's "truth" is pointless.

Wesley's doctrine of Scripture, then, relates far more to *forming* believers in the image of Christ, nurturing a life in loving relationship with God and one's neighbor, than to *informing* them about God and the world. It isn't meant to be a storehouse of propositions, assent to which assures that believers either gain or maintain a favorable relationship with God.

But thinking that John Wesley cared little about scripturally based doctrine would be a mistake. Scripture contains "the whole will of God." It instructs us in "those grand, fundamental doctrines [of] original sin, justification by faith, the new birth, [and] inward and outward holiness."[12] All doctrine must have its clear grounding in Scripture. In his essay "A Roman Catechism," Wesley writes, "We read in Scripture of 'the faith once delivered to the saints;' (Jude 1:3;) and 'all' or the whole 'Scripture is profitable for doctrine. . . . (2 Tim. iii. 16, 17.)"[13] The end of all doctrine is our relationship with God. The conjunction is essential: "We then establish the law, when we declare every part of it, every commandment contained therein, not only in its full literal sense, but likewise in its spiritual meaning; not only with regard to the outward actions, which it either forbids or enjoins, but also with respect to the inward principle, to the thoughts, desires, and intents of the heart."[14]

So, for Wesley, doctrine is far more than a body of propositional truths to be believed and obeyed. They are the structure of Christian faith that must become incarnate in those whom God's love transforms.

Wesley's instructions for reading Scripture continue:

If you desire to read the Scriptures in such a manner as may most effectually answer this end, would it not be advisable, (1.) To set apart a little time, if you can, every morning and evening for that purpose? (2.) At each time, if you have leisure, to read a chapter out of the Old and one out of the New Testament; if you cannot do this, to take a single chapter, or a part of one? (3.) To read this with a single eye, to know the whole will of God, and a fixed resolution to do it? In order to know his will, you should, (4.) Have a constant eye to the analogy of faith, the connection and harmony there is between those grand, fundamental doctrines, original sin, justification by faith, the new birth, inward and outward holiness: (5.) Serious and earnest prayer should be constantly used before we consult the oracles of God; seeing "Scripture can only be understood through the same Spirit whereby it was given."[15] Our reading should likewise be closed with prayer, that what we read may be written on our hearts: (6.) It might also be of use, if, while we read, we were frequently to pause, and examine ourselves by what we read, both with regard to our hearts and lives. . . . And whatever light you then receive should be used to the uttermost, and that immediately. Let there be no delay. Whatever you resolve, begin to execute the first moment you can. So shall you find this word to be indeed the power of God unto present and eternal salvation.[16]

We see even wider dimensions of Wesley's doctrine of Scripture in his instructions for reading the Scripture to nurture the love relationship with God that results in transforming one's inner nature and outward behavior. Because Scripture is a primary means of grace, Wesley urged a daily discipline[17] of immersing oneself in the Scripture.[18] Far more than "checking off" a discipline designed to win God's favor, properly studying the Bible first means unreservedly offering oneself to God: "To read . . .

with a single eye,[19] to know the whole will of God, and a fixed resolution to do it."

It might be thought that here Wesley is thinking of a set of propositions that are to be persistently followed. However, this would be reading into Wesley the concept of truth as propositional. Perhaps Wesley's injunction can best be understood by using a biblical example. In Exod. 19, Moses and the people of Israel have finally arrived at Mount Sinai. God calls to Moses from the mountain and gives him a message for the people. "You have seen what I did to the Egyptians, and how I bore you on eagles' wings and brought you to myself. Now therefore, if you obey my voice and keep my covenant, you shall be my treasured possession out of all the peoples. Indeed, the whole earth is mine, but you shall be for me a priestly kingdom and a holy nation" (19:4-6). Moses gives God's message to the elders who, presumably, relayed it to the tribes. Then "the people all answered as one: 'Everything that the LORD has spoken we will do'" (v. 8). Notice that no specific commandments or ordinances have yet been given. Instead, God first invites the people into a living relationship with him ("I . . . brought you to myself. . . . you shall be my treasured possession"). He calls for their unconditional allegiance to that relationship even before they know all it will entail. Obeying the specifics of the covenant is subsidiary, or subsequent, to relationship. This is what Wesley means when he instructs us to "read . . . with a single eye." It involves directing one's whole self toward God, loving him with all one's heart, soul, mind, and strength so completely that one's only desire is to know the fullness of God's will ("to know the whole will of God") in order to fulfill it ("a fixed resolution to do it") irrespective of what it might be.

Scripture frames "the whole will of God," for Wesley, within the context of the human condition and God's action— "those grand, fundamental doctrines, original sin, justification by faith, the new birth, inward and outward holiness."

34

The heart of Wesley's doctrine of Scripture emerges in the fifth directive: "Scripture can only be understood through the same Spirit whereby it was given." Here Wesley seems to be giving a succinct exegesis of 2 Pet. 1:20-21: "No prophecy of scripture is a matter of one's own interpretation, because no prophecy ever came by human will, but men and women moved by the Holy Spirit spoke from God." Wesley clearly believed Scripture came through persons who were moved by the Holy Spirit. His doctrine of inspiration, however, extends beyond the inspiration of the writers. He infers that if, as Peter says, Scripture is not "a matter of one's own interpretation," then how is it to be interpreted? Peter implies that interpretation or comprehension, like the Scripture itself, must also be the work of the Holy Spirit. This is why Wesley counsels that "serious and earnest prayer should be constantly used before we consult the oracles of God" (instruction 5 above). The nature of such prayer is clear: "Scripture can only be understood through the same Spirit whereby it was given." Prayer receptively and responsively opens oneself to the Holy Spirit. The "circuit" of inspiration is complete when the reader allows the Spirit, who inspires the text, to illumine the text for the reader's transformation. Wesley makes the circuit clear: "Our reading should likewise be closed with prayer, that what we read may be written on our hearts." Hence, what it means for Scripture to be "inspired" is lifeless apart from the inner and outer "transformation" of the whole person.

This transformative dimension is seen in his injunction, "frequently to pause, and examine ourselves by what we read, both with regard to our hearts and lives." Thomas Merton echoes Wesley: "The basic claim made by the Bible for the Word of God is not so much that it is to be blindly accepted because of God's authority, but that it is recognized by its transforming and liberating power."[20] Or, as noted above, "God manifests himself not in information but in life-giving power."[21] When the Bible is understood primarily as a body of propositional truths to be understood, accepted, and affirmed by believers, all too often the essential transformational dimension vanishes.

A summary of Wesley's doctrine of Scripture is the Word that became flesh in Jesus of Nazareth also became "text," providing a vehicle for a transforming encounter with God, so that he who is the Word might through the Holy Spirit become flesh in us.

Charles Wesley voiced this incarnational doctrine of Scripture in his hymns. Here is an example.

> *Come, Holy Ghost, our hearts inspire,*
> *Let us thine influence prove:*
> *Source of the old prophetic fire,*
> *Fountain of life and love.*

> *Come Holy Ghost, for moved by thee*
> *The prophets wrote and spoke;*
> *Unlock the truth, thyself the key,*
> *Unseal the sacred book.*

> *Expand thy wings, celestial Dove,*
> *Brood o'er our nature's night;*
> *On our disordered spirits move,*
> *And let there now be light.*

> *God, through himself, we then shall know*
> *If thou within us shine,*
> *And sound with all thy saints below,*
> *The depths of love divine.*[22]

In harmony with his brother John, Charles says the Holy Spirit is the key that "unlock[s] the truth" and "unseal[s] the sacred book," the end of which is reformation: "Brood o'er our nature's night; / On our disordered spirits move, / And let there now be light." This is the unique work of the Spirit of God, not of a written text.

The inseparable connection between the experiential knowledge of God and the Scripture is found in another hymn:

> *While in thy word we search for thee,*
> *(We search with trembling awe!)*
> *Open our eyes, and let us see*
> *The wonders of thy law.*[23]

In this context it must be noted that "the wonders of thy law" culminates the "search for thee." We see that the "law" is not a body of propositional truths but the essential nature of God himself. For the Wesley brothers the role of Scripture was not the appropriation of propositional truths but the actualization of a relationship of loving union with God for the sake of the world.

Perhaps nothing better epitomizes the role of Scripture for Wesley than the following hymn:

> *When quiet in my house I sit,*
> *Thy book be my companion still,*
> *My joy thy sayings to repeat,*
> *Talk o'er the records of thy will,*
> *And search the oracles divine,*
> *Till every heartfelt word be mine.*
>
> *O may the gracious words divine*
> *Subject of all my converse be:*
> *So will the Lord his follower join,*
> *And walk and talk himself with me;*
> *So shall my heart his presence prove,*
> *And burn with everlasting love.*[24]

It is no wonder, then, that Wesley described himself as "*homo unius libri,*" that is, "a man of one book."[25] Although he was widely read in the literature of his own day and in the writings of the early church, for Wesley the Scripture was the primary means (after Christ) by which God reveals himself to humanity.[26]

Conclusion

Although we have explored serious differences between a fundamentalist and a Wesleyan doctrine of Scripture, it would be a grave error to imply that fundamentalists are any less interested in Christian discipleship than are Wesleyans. Like Wesleyans, fundamentalists are carefully attentive to the redeeming work of Jesus Christ, to the importance of being born anew by the Spirit of God, and to a life of Christian discipleship.

But when it comes to the primary nature and role of the Bible, there are, as we have seen, major differences. For fundamentalism, the Bible itself, with its comprehensive and rationally accessible inerrant divine truths or propositions, is the depository and residence of inspiration. The Bible and its truths are the primary objects of attention.

For John Wesley, for whom the Scriptures are truly the Word of God, the primary role of Scripture resides not in the text as divine information but in the Holy Spirit's use of it for a transforming encounter with the risen Christ, the true Word of God. Christ as the encountered Redeemer, not the Bible, is of primary interest and importance. The Bible is the means the Holy Spirit uses for inner regeneration and the sanctified life.

WHY IT MATTERS
(Chapter 2)

Clair MacMillan, DD

During three discussion sessions, fifteen laypersons and I examined the practical implications of the contrast Dr. Mulholland draws between fundamentalist and Wesleyan ways of understanding the nature and purpose of the Bible. We understood him to be saying that fundamentalists tend to view Scripture as a body of unquestionable divinely given information that must be accepted as something of a rule book for safe Christian living. It is meant to be authoritative in all the topics it addresses. Wesleyans, on the other hand, believe that the primary purpose of the Bible is to glorify God and form the people of God in the image of Christ. Thus its focus is not on issuing propositional truths about God and the world. Formation, not information, is its defining goal.

Wesleyans accordingly believe that the authority of Scripture is centered on its Spirit-inspired ability to nurture Jesus' disciples in loving relationships with God and neighbor. The writers of the Bible tell us how to live in these right relationships and do not attempt to set forth a vast body of knowledge—historical and scientific—that Christians must unquestionably accept.

When the question was asked, "Why does this distinction between fundamentalists and Wesleyans matter?" our discussion participants responded that Dr. Mulholland had helped them understand that God gave us the Bible to show us the way to salvation and to a right relationship with him. The purpose of Scripture is to warn us against the many ways our love for God and neighbor can be impeded by yielding to temptation. Faithfully reading the Bible, as several participants observed, alerts us to sins of which we might be unaware, including the temptation to lose hope in God's faithfulness, to neglect eternal life, and to begin living just for today.

The distinction made in the chapter matters because it helps us realize that the Bible's truth is primarily its faithful testimony to God who is the world's Creator and Redeemer. Its truth has nothing to do with providing accurate scientific information. Its truth doesn't lie in its ability to tell us "everything that was going on" in all eras of human history. The Wesleyan way of approaching the Bible sets us free to take seriously the humanity of the Bible's authors. They were free to use literary genres, such as poetry and parables, and literary devices, such as analogy and hyperbole, in service to God's will, which shines through all these methods. That, Dr. Mulholland makes clear, is the center of the Bible's authority.

Our discussion group recognized that for Wesleyans the Bible is absolutely trustworthy because it accurately reveals God's will for humankind in all matters concerning our salvation and practice. The Wesleyan approach to Scripture is important because it demonstrates that the Bible uniquely and reliably reveals God's desire and plan for human salvation.

The Bible, as Dr. Mulholland points out, teaches us the nature of God as revealed in the person of Jesus Christ. It explains what it means to be alienated from God because of sin. But it also bears witness to God's plan for redeeming humankind—a plan God fulfilled in his Son, Jesus Christ. The Bible's defining purpose is fulfilled when persons are reconciled to God through Jesus Christ and experience the Holy Spirit's witness to their adoption as sons and daughters of God. Rising to live transformed lives, Christians know with certainty through the Holy Spirit that the Bible's witness to Christ is true.

▪ 3 ▪
THE BIBLE, CREATION, AND SCIENCE

Robert Branson, PhD

■ Isn't it odd how some conversations stick in your memory? As a high school junior I took a required course in biology. One spring afternoon, while my pastor and I were walking through the partially constructed addition to our church, I explained what we were being taught in biology. My pastor responded, "Bob, you will either have to believe the Bible or believe science." My unspoken response was: "If that is the choice, I know who will win. There must be a better option."

With modern science progressing in so many areas, if a person is forced to choose between science and the Bible, most informed people will choose science. But is this a necessary choice? Why would the God who has so grandly written his signature in creation and who has made known his redemptive purpose in Scripture place the two testimonies in opposition?

Perhaps the forced "choice" results from a fundamental misunderstanding and misinterpretation of the two records. Science peers into the cosmic record by using refined technology. It uses increasingly accurate techniques to explore cosmology, geology, and biology. Most of the results are readily available to the public. Many scientists who are Christians concur that nature's records are being correctly examined.[1] So, too, orthodox biblical scholars study the Scriptures with the utmost care.[2] They recognize that God's creation of the world is a theme that runs throughout the Old and New Testaments (see Job 38–39; Ps. 104; Prov. 8:22-31; John 1:1-5; Col. 1:15-17). The Bible eloquently proclaims that God is the Creator of all that exists. Must these two stories conflict? Must one story suffocate the other?

Many Christians believe there is an irreconcilable conflict between how scientists read the natural order and what the Bible teaches about creation and human existence. The conflict arises largely from what they think the opening chapters of the book of Genesis teach, particularly chapter 1. They see those chapters as intending to provide an accurate scientific and historical account of how creation happened; if scientists disagree in any way, they are simply wrong. But how can these Christians be so confident they have correctly understood the first chapters of Genesis? How can they be so certain that a scientific account of creation is what those chapters offer? Are modern science and the Genesis story of creation actually combatants? Or is there a more accurate way to understand the message of Genesis that makes conflict unnecessary? To be faithful to the Scriptures, we must use our best available tools to learn what Genesis actually teaches.

In many places the Bible speaks of God as the Creator. In this chapter we will concentrate on the first chapter of Genesis. Our examination will have two parts. In the *first* section we will examine some of the *presuppositions* or underlying ideas that should come into play when discussing the relationship between what science teaches and what the book of Genesis says about creation. The *second section* examines three different ways Christians have approached the relationship between modern science and what Gen. 1:1–2:3 says about God as Creator. A fourth position exists but will not be treated here. It is an atheistic view that judges the Bible as totally irrelevant to the natural order. The positions we will examine are as follows: (1) concordance, which interprets the Bible so as to make it *fit the discoveries of science*; (2) young-earth creationism, which forces *science to fit the Bible*; and (3) a separatist position that sees science and the Bible as representing "separate spheres of authoritative discourse."[3] Far from trying to make the Bible address modern science, this position holds that Gen. 1 is a distinct theological statement set within ancient Israel's cultural context. Genesis doesn't raise the questions scientists raise. This position is generally advocated by current biblical scholars. But it is not well known among laypersons and clergy.

Part One: Examining the Presuppositions

Several presuppositions underlie discussions about the relationship between what the Bible teaches regarding creation and what the natural sciences teach about the age and history of the universe.

The *first* presupposition is that the Scriptures are inspired by God and are hence trustworthy. Wesleyans firmly agree, so long as we understand that (1) God used humans to record the Scriptures and that (2) God did not override or ignore the personalities and cultures of the biblical writers. God willingly accepted these "limitations" or tools, yet fully communicated his message of creation, providence, and salvation. Wesleyans believe the Bible is inerrant in all things pertaining to Christian faith and practice.[4] But they also recognize the Bible's human qualities, just as they affirm Jesus' full deity while also embracing his full humanity—God incarnate.

Early in church history some people known as docetists (from the Greek *dokesis*, meaning "appearance" or "semblance") taught that Jesus was fully divine, but only appeared to be human. His sufferings and death were mere appearances. By denying Jesus' humanity the docetists robbed him of his ability to identify with us humans, and hence to be our Redeemer. The early church righty condemned the docetists as heretics and affirmed Jesus' full deity and humanity in one person. His humanity was essential to his being the Redeemer. The church recognized that if Jesus was truly human, then his human knowledge was also limited. For example, he did not know the time of the kingdom's consummation (Mark 13:32). He spoke about things then commonly accepted but which have since been discovered to be incorrect (4:31).

There are still Christians who find it difficult to accept Jesus' humanity, just as they find it difficult to accept the Bible's humanity. Those who insist that the Bible must be divine or inerrant in every single detail misrepresent it just as the docetists misrepresented Jesus. They obscure the clear biblical evidence that God did not hesitate to use fallible and historically/culturally situated human instruments when telling us who he is and what he wills for his people and creation. The biblical writers were inspired by God to faithfully record God's mighty deeds of salvation. But they also reflected the worldview of ancient Israelite culture, with its roots in the broader ancient Near East (ANE). Why would this not be true? Recognizing this fact is a threat only to those who approach the Scriptures as the docetists approached Jesus.

Second, the Creator God revealed in the Bible is just and honest. Lying or misrepresenting reality is contrary to his nature. Two companion truths support this presupposition. (1) God has not falsified the Scriptures so that people would be led astray. The Bible speaks plainly to the matter of salvation. But interpretations of texts must take account of their cultural background, immediate context, the kinds of literature they are (e.g., parables, psalms), and their purpose. When the psalmist says, "He [God] has established the world: it shall never be moved" (93:1*c*), he is not making a statement about geology (Israelites were painfully aware of earthquakes) or astronomy. Instead, in poetic form and exalted language the psalmist praises God's sovereignty and faithfulness to his creation. Contrary to how the medieval church interpreted the text, the psalm doesn't claim that the earth is the center of the solar system or that it doesn't rotate on its axis. The psalm's purpose has to be observed. (2) God has not falsified the natural record of the universe. When read faithfully by the sciences of geology, biology, physics, and astronomy, the natural record gives a true description of God's creative processes. Some people say that although the natural order seems to contain evidence of processes occurring over very long periods of time (e.g., simple life-forms first appearing on earth approximately 1.8 billion years ago), God actually created the universe in a very brief span. This implies that God is misleading.

Third, because God created the universe, he has full knowledge of the processes he used. As it stands, the statement is correct. But the next step is flawed: therefore the accounts of creation given in Genesis must be scientifically and historically accurate.[5] True, God certainly knows the processes of creation. But what sense would it make to relay a modern scientific account of those processes to people who had no frame of reference for receiving them?

The Old Testament picture of the universe is prescientific, similar to that held by other cultures in the ANE. That worldview even predated the second-century Ptolemaic (to-le-may-ic) belief that the earth is the center of the universe.[6] (The chapter's last section will develop the ANE worldview more fully.)

The modern understanding of science and history are recent developments. Nicolaus Copernicus (1473–1543) published his work describing a heliocentric cosmology in the mid-sixteenth century. Gregor Mendel (1822-84), father of modern genetics, published his work on inherited traits in the mid-nineteenth century. Hermann Joseph Muller (1890–1967) conducted his genetics experiments in the early twentieth century. Our current view of the world and life in it is very different from ancient times. If God had used modern explanations to tell ancient Israelites how he created, he would have been using language they could not have grasped. Furthermore, future developments in science will probably make much of our current knowledge obsolete. It is one thing to say we believe God is the Creator. It is quite another to say that in Scripture God described with scientific accuracy "when" and "how" he created. The error of imposing our modern understanding of the universe on ancient writers of the Bible should be obvious.

Part Two: Various Assessments of Genesis and Modern Science

Now let's examine three different estimates of what the relationship between Gen. 1 and modern science should be.

1. The Concordance Approach

This approach seeks to make the Bible comply with modern science so that the two are in concordance or agreement.

A student who had been reading about Charles Darwin once asked me if the days mentioned in Gen. 1 should be interpreted as geological ages. Doing so, the student thought, might reconcile the six days of creation discussed in Gen. 1:1–2:3 with Darwin's theory of evolution. I answered, "Yes, they could be. But the problem is that no one today accepts Darwin's theory just as he stated it." Recent knowledge about genetics has modified Darwin's original theory. Now we deal with Neo-Darwinism. Because our knowledge continues to expand, reconciling science and the Bible would require repeatedly revising the Bible to agree with the most recent scientific theory.

The concordance position is not new. Thomas Burnet (1635–1715) in his *Sacred Theory of the Universe* (1681) treated Gen. 1 "as a textbook of cosmology and geology." He followed the path of Copernicus by maintaining that interpreting the Bible correctly must depend on a proper understanding of science.[7] Burnet's work illustrates the first problem resulting from the concordance approach. Scripture becomes subservient to science. We cannot know what the Bible means until science instructs us.

Robert C. Newman and Herman J. Eckelmann Jr., in their book *Genesis One and the Origin of the Earth* (1977), use the concordance approach. The first part of their book reviews the contemporary scientific understanding of how the earth was created. The last section attempts to interpret Gen. 1 in a way that agrees or concords with the scientific data.

The authors think Gen. 1:1–2:3 describes the creation process as seen in a vision by someone standing on the earth and limited by an earthly perspective.[8] The observer sees that the world is created in six twenty-four-hour periods. But what this person doesn't know is that creation was largely occurring in between the days. The six days were not immediately consecutive.[9] What happened between the days agrees with what contemporary science teaches about the age of the world and life on earth.[10]

This way of making Genesis conform to modern science illustrates the second problem associated with concordance. The biblical text is interpreted (twisted) to correspond to what contemporary science requires. The Bible is stripped of its independent voice and forced to speak the language of modern science, a language unknown to the Bible's original recipients and writers.

Another problem associated with concordance involves the question, "With which science is Genesis supposed to agree?" During the seventeenth and eighteenth centuries a mechanical view of the universe based on Newtonian physics prevailed. It was thought that all creation functioned in accordance with mechanical laws such as characterize fine watches and machines. But today's view of the universe is quite different. It is shaped by biological evolution and quantum physics. It is quite likely that new discoveries will reshape our current perceptions. Should our understanding of what Genesis teaches be subjected to repeated revisions based upon the latest discoveries in science?

2. Young-Earth Creationism

Young-earth creationism (YEC) forces science to comply with Genesis. It is institutionally supported by the Institute for Creation Research and the Creation Research Society.

By accepting the chronology and genealogies of the Bible as historically accurate,[11] young-earth creationism concludes that the universe is very young, approximately six thousand to ten thousand years old. In six twenty-four-hour days God created everything, including the universe and all vegetative and biological life. A mature tree was created with all its rings, making it appear much older. When God created light on the first day, "these light-waves traversing space from the heavenly bodies to the earth were energized even before the heavenly bodies themselves in order to provide the light for the first three days."[12] At the end of six days the universe was mature.

A colleague said that as a first-year graduate student in biology he looked forward to a "creation science" debate to be conducted at his university. The guest was Duane Gish, an advocate of the young-earth position. His opponent from the university was a paleontologist who was also a Christian. My colleague had been raised in a Christian home and had faithfully attended church. He anticipated that the debate would demonstrate how belief in a six twenty-four-hour-day creation could be defended by scientific evidence. As the debate proceeded, my colleague began to realize that the guest did not actually understand the science of biology. While the presentation might have sounded knowledgeable to the uninformed, those grounded in biological science were disappointed, even repulsed.

While supporters of the concordance approach try to *correlate the biblical account of creation with science*, exponents of YEC begin with the Bible and attempt to *correlate science with the Bible*. A common-sense approach based on Scottish realism (see chap. 5) forms the basis for why YEC advocates value Gen. 1 as "literal history," an accurate physical and temporal account of what actually happened at creation. They claim (erroneously) not to interpret the text but simply to accept what it says. Any competing interpretation is rejected as mythological or faithless.

Only after humanity in the garden sinned against God did death enter and creation suffer corruption. No humans or animals suffered death before then.[13] Therefore, all fossil records that appear to be millions of years old actually result from recent catastrophic events, especially the biblical flood. The fossil record was not formed over millions of years but "over a period of months or years."[14] The mechanism for the fossil deposits and for much of the present shape of the earth was the flood.[15] Only subsequent to the flood did a natural uniformity of change begin.[16] Human history and the earth's structure were begun and shaped by three great events: creation, the fall, and the flood.

How then are the results of science fitted into this interpretation of the biblical account? Creationists almost exclusively accept the Baconian method of science: "experimental observation."[17] Francis Bacon (1561–1626) established the inductive method that forms the basis of much scientific research today. However, creationists often want to rule out the use of scientific theory and models, such as evolution, because they say the theories and models are not sufficiently based on factual observation. (1) They reject the standard way scientists decide the age of rocks as unreliable.[18] (2) They say given that the light trails from stars were created on the first day—three days before the heavenly bodies were created—the results of astronomy cannot be relied upon. (3) The earth was created already bearing the marks of age.

Theories such as evolution and uniformitarianism (laws that operate in the universe today have always operated) are rejected as false. The reason given by YEC supporters is that such theories do not agree with how creationists interpret Scripture.

Why do many scientists who are Christian object to how advocates of YEC use the Bible to explain creation? Primarily because creationists habitually reject or distort the findings of reputable science. Davis Young's *Christianity and the Age of the Earth* (1982) was written to demonstrate the flood's failure to account for the present stratigraphy (a branch of geology that studies the layering of rocks). Not only does Young defend the modern results of geology, but he also exposes the errors of the YEC position. In particular he shows, contrary to creationist objections, the validity of radiometric dating.[19] Howard J. Van Till has demonstrated the integrity of contemporary natural science as a discipline that investigates the wonders of God's creation.[20] Darrel Falk (2004), Richard G.

Colling (2004), and Francis S. Collins (2006) have shown the valid basis for biological evolution.

In the final analysis, YEC does not legitimately deal with modern science. It either distorts it or dismisses it without basis. This neither honors God and the Bible nor treats with integrity the findings of science.

3. The Cosmology of Genesis 1

If trying to interpret the Bible to *fit the discoveries of science* (concordance) distorts the biblical text, and if trying to *force science to fit an interpretation of the Bible* (YEC) distorts science, what other option is there? A third approach is to read the biblical text as it was originally addressed to an Israelite audience. This is not as simple as it sounds. A modern reader must first step out of his or her own culture and step back in time some three thousand years. We must ask, what was the culture like at that time? How did the people view their world? What are the theological questions the text addresses?

As we answer these questions, carefully observe not only the cultural similarities but also the important distinctions being made between the one true God who created the world and the false gods worshipped by the surrounding cultures. The distinctions, not the similarities, form the point of concentration.

Howard J. Van Till has correctly diagnosed our task:

The Christian church has long confessed that even the most humble reader of the Bible will be capable of grasping all that is necessary for hearing God's call to repentance, his offer of redemption, his assurance of fatherly care, and his will for faithful service. Nonetheless, we also recognize that the Bible is an unfathomably rich reserve of God's disclosures in a form that is sometimes obscure and culturally alien to us and that it therefore demands continuing and intensive study by those who are specially called and trained to do so.[21]

The phrase "culturally alien to us" is significant. We are somewhat familiar with the setting of the New Testament (NT), which was steeped in Greco-Roman culture. Even though the honor-shame culture of the first century differs from our Western guilt-based culture, the NT message of redemption still comes through clearly. This is less true for much of the Old Testament (OT). Often the cultural background, the various tribes and nations, and the customs are alien to us. Translators place explanatory notes in our Bibles, and we often consult commentaries to understand an OT text's setting. Why is our understanding of the OT so different from that of the New? Why have we usually been able to comprehend the Greek and Latin writings but not those of the ANE?

To answer these questions, we need to review some Western history. The Greek and Roman cultures that form the NT background have been largely passed down to us by Western culture. They form the basis for many of our traditions and ways of thinking. But the culture of the ANE, of which Israel was a part, was largely lost to history. Apart from the Bible itself, until the nineteenth century scholars were not able to read the literature of the ANE, either of the Egyptians or of the peoples of Mesopotamia. During Napoleon's invasion of Egypt (1798–1801) a French soldier found a stone near the village of Rosetta on which was inscribed a decree of Ptolemy V (reigned 204–181 BC) in three languages: ancient Egyptian hieroglyphs, demotic (later) Egyptian, and ancient Greek. Because scholars could read the Greek, they used it as a key to decipher the Egyptian hieroglyphs. For the first time in the modern era the many inscriptions found in tombs and monuments could be read. Insight into the culture with which Abraham, Jacob, Joseph, Moses, and the Israelites interacted was obtained.

At about the same time scholars began the more difficult task of reading the inscriptions the Persian king Darius I (550–486 BC) had carved on the face of the Behistun cliff, located in modern Iran. It was inscribed in the cuneiform script of three languages: Old Persian, Elamite, and Babylonian. Not until the mid-nineteenth century were the texts finally deciphered. For the last 150 years scholars have been studying the literature of both Babylon and Assyria, piecing together a mosaic of how the people who were the ancestors of Abraham, and thus all his descendants, lived and thought.

A third significant archaeological find occurred in 1929 when the ancient Canaanite city of Ugarit, located on the eastern shore of the Mediterranean, was discovered. The royal archives were unearthed, and in 1933 Cyrus Gordon published a grammar of the language. As the texts were read, we began to understand who the gods of the Canaanites were—Baal, Anat, Asherah, El, Dagon—and why the Israelites were attracted to them.

Israel was located on the eastern shore of the Mediterranean and thus on the trade routes between Egypt and Mesopotamia. They experienced the continual flow of trade crossing their land. Also, Israel always confessed that their historic roots were not in Canaan but in Mesopotamia (stories of Abraham and Jacob). For four centuries Israel lived in Egypt. These roots and constant contact with the major ANE cultures shaped Israel's worldview. The literature of the ANE is voluminous. But its creation texts are most important for understanding how Israel viewed the world and what made its theological understanding unique.[22]

The first statement of Gen. 1 proclaims there is one God, and only one God, who is responsible for creation. This seems obvious to us, but the ANE nations worshipped many gods. Israel was making a startling claim. In cuneiform writings—*Enuma Elish* and *Atrahasis*—darkness upon waters preceded the creation of the world. Where did the light come from?

In Gen. 1:2, in keeping with other ANE texts, God began the process of ordering creation by working with the chaotic waters that surged back and forth in total darkness. Genesis gives no explanation of how these waters came to be; their existence is taken for granted. God called forth light in the midst of darkness (v. 3). This was not the light of the stars and sun. Ancient people thought light emanated from the gods. For instance, Ps. 104, a creation psalm, proclaims: "O

LORD my God, you are very great. You are clothed with honor and majesty, wrapped in light as with a garment" (vv. 1*b*-2*a*). Israel accepted the ANE concept but theologically reformed it by proclaiming that the light comes from the one true God. By calling the light "day" and the darkness "night" (Gen. 1:5), God established the function of light and darkness, to measure time, "for time is the invariable alteration between periods of light and periods of darkness."[23]

Before the earth could be inhabited, the cosmic waters had to be separated. In *Enuma Elish* the Babylonian god Marduk separated the waters above from the waters below by placing the body of the defeated Tiamat between them. By contrast, for Israel, on day two (vv. 6-8) God separated the waters by placing a solid barrier, a dome (NRSV) or firmament (KJV), between them. The cosmic waters represented a continual threat. In the flood (6:5–8:22) the barrier was breached so that the inhabitable earth was destroyed (7:11). The function of the dome was to provide space for the inhabitants of the earth and to control precipitation and thus weather.[24]

On day three (1:9-13) God established the seas and the dry land. The function of the land was to bring forth vegetation, which would provide food for both animals and humans. Thus on the first three days God created time, weather, and food, which "are the foundation of life."[25] The next three days complement the first three by "filling" what has already been ordered.

Preparation	Filling
Day One—Light/Time	Day Four—Stars, Sun, Moon
Day Two—Dome/Space/Weather	Day Five—Birds and Sea Creatures
Day Three—Land and Vegetation	Day Six—Animals and Humans

When the writer described God's action of creating the heavenly bodies on day four (vv. 14-19), the words were chosen carefully. The "greater light" is not called the "sun." In Hebrew the word for sun, *shemesh*, is also the name of the Canaanite sun god. The writer guarded against any thought that there might be another god. The lights functioned as signs to humanity of seasons, days, and years. The sun, moon, and stars are not divine powers that control human destiny.

The lights were hung upon the dome created on day two. These verses illustrate that Israel's concept of the cosmos was different from our scientific assessment. We understand that the stars are older than the earth and that vast distances separate them from us and from each other. The Israelites believed that first a dome had to be established from which the lights could be suspended. All attempts to explain these verses scientifically flounder at this point. The account is not wrong or in error. The Israelites accepted the common view of the ANE and used it to express their belief that one God established an inhabitable world. We commonly state that the sun rises and sets, that the moon shines. We use this language metaphorically and don't intend it to be scientifically correct. Two centuries ago Westerners compared the universe to a well-functioning machine as their way of understanding the world. We no longer use that language. But we can easily see how culture provides a metaphor for talking about the physical world we observe. We can also see how metaphors change as our understanding of the universe changes, without fundamentally changing the truth being signified.

On day five (vv. 20-23) God filled the sky with birds and the seas with fish. They were the "functionaries" who fulfilled their roles in the space given to them.[26] Similarly on day six (vv. 24-31) land animals and humans were assigned their space and functions. However, Israel understood the functions of humans differently. In the other nations of the ANE, humans were created to serve the gods, to provide their food and perform labors too menial for gods. But in Genesis no such low estate is assigned to humans. Instead, the earth was prepared, not for God, but for humanity created in God's image. Humanity represents God to the rest of creation and has the task of subduing creation, that is, to participate with God by bringing order to it, making it fruitful and productive. Humanity is given charge to rule over the creation as vice-regent, subject to and answerable to the Creator.

Conclusion

The theological message of Gen. 1 has always been clear. Only one God has given order to the world. He is the sovereign Deity who is not part of the universe. But his majesty and glory can be seen in it by those of faith. Humans have been given a preeminent place in creation. They are supposed to represent God and continue bringing order to the world by making it productive and fruitful. The literary structure of the text— three days of preparation followed by three days of filling—has been noted by scholars over the centuries. But only recently, perhaps by divine plan, have they been able to read the ANE texts. This happened as scientists were exploring the vast universe and deciphering its age and astonishing structure. Being able to read the ancient texts has made it possible to understand as never before the intellectual culture Israel shared with its neighbors. But this has also richly clarified how significantly Israel's faith diverged from neighboring cultures.

Absent this knowledge we have often read into the text our own cultural understandings. In the Middle Ages, not only was the earth thought to be the center of the cosmos but also humanity the center of God's special concern. During the Newtonian era the universe was thought to be a vast machine running with precise accuracy. God was the ultimate "Watchmaker." More recently, we have tried to make Gen. 1 comply with succeeding scientific theories, expanding the days into long ages and reading into the creative acts cosmic activities we now believe to have happened. Or we have tried to reinterpret science so as to make it comply with our own interpretations of the text.

By reading Gen. 1 in its cultural context, reading it as the Israelites did, we free the text to speak with its own powerful voice. We do not need science to validate its message. Nor do we consider its message irrelevant to modern times. Science can describe the processes God used to bring the universe into existence and to make the earth habitable. This should expand our wonder. The Bible speaks of the God who has ordered the creation and of his redemptive activity. These are two distinct but not unrelated domains or areas of truth. We cannot balkanize or segregate the two. They must intersect. When the psalmist proclaimed, "A thousand years in your sight are like yesterday when it is past" (Ps. 90:4), he was saying that time does not limit God. And when the psalmist said, "If I ascend to heaven, you are there; if I make my bed in Sheol, you are there" (139:8), he was announcing that God is not limited by space. Science has enlarged our concepts of space and time and by so doing enlarged our understanding of the sovereignty and majesty of the God who rules over all of creation and who in Christ became incarnate as the world's Redeemer (John 1:1-5; 3:16).

WHY IT MATTERS
(Chapter 3)

Bethany Hull Somers, MDiv

Trying to capture the big picture of what Dr. Branson has presented leads to the following observations and practical implications.

First, "In the beginning . . . God" (Gen. 1:1). The first words of the Bible provide the framework for the story of God that follows. The Bible is God's story and the story of God's people. Throughout its contents the story has different functions. At times it is history, at other times prophecy; sometimes instruction and at other times inspiration. The story is all these and more. To be faithful to the whole story, we must accept an invitation to participate in the mysterious and amazing life of God.

Invitation to a mystery is a funny thing. It rules out the notion that we have everything figured out in advance. It disallows neat and tidy lines, and black-and-white generalizations. The invitation requires that we remain open and ready for adventure, ready to be surprised by God. It means from beginning to end that we look to God alone.

Unfortunately, there are voices in Christ's church that challenge this openness and readiness for adventure in God's story. Though well intended, they draw sharp lines and make sweeping claims about how the Bible should be understood.

It is difficult for me as a parish minister to navigate between well-meaning parishioners who embrace fundamentalism and the challenge fundamentalism poses to exploring the whole story of God. I watch as fundamentalism obstructs a full engagement with the Bible's riches. At heart, fundamentalism represents a sincere desire to be faithful to God's Word and to Christian faith and practice.

The problem is that good intentions do not necessarily lead to sound theology. Sincerity might not result in faithfully exploring the whole story of God.

Being faithful to the Christian story means being open to the love of the risen Christ. It rules out arguing about the minutiae of Scripture or insisting on how it should be understood in all its details. Faithfulness to God's story and to the Bible is fulfilled in submission to the love and victory of Christ.

Debates about how God chose to create and about what the Bible says regarding creation illustrate good intentions that are harmful, unnecessarily divisive, and misrepresentative of the story of God and his people.

The truth is that none of us know for certain how God created the world. Our certainty comes from what we think the Bible says. But the book of Genesis was written long *after* creation occurred. As Dr. Branson has shown, Genesis intentionally employs the language and some of the concepts of an ancient, prescientific culture for which modern cosmology would have made no sense at all.

Moreover, among Christians there is a wide range of ideas about creation. In my congregation, for example, some people believe God created in six twenty-four-hour days. Others think God could have used the process of evolution to create all that is "good." Respect for these diverse opinions tempers our conversations and our interpretations of the Bible. Because our conversations concentrate on "who created" and not on "how God created" we can engage in respectful dialogue.

Second, any interpretation of the Bible that hinders the Holy Spirit's witness to the gospel of Jesus Christ or that diverts our full attention from discipleship should be avoided. Many of the debates that characterize fundamentalism distract attention from the gospel, from Christian witness, and from the life of Christian holiness. Fundamentalist arguments about the Bible can cause us to miss important opportunities to share God's love with others. Fundamentalism establishes boundaries never drawn by Jesus in the Gospels. Embracing and expounding fundamentalism will likely cause us to avoid certain people because they reject the artificial boundaries fundamentalism imposes on the Bible. As a result, God's grace will be shortchanged—grace that could otherwise be working through us.

Instead of placing our confidence in a questionable interpretation of the Bible, let us place it in the Holy Spirit who uses the Scriptures to convince persons that Jesus is Lord. He is the One who does all things well.

Being open to what the Holy Spirit wants to accomplish might require us to enter arenas we would never have imagined, to befriend persons who might have made our grandmothers cringe, and to meet persons at their points of need. Our guide is not a doubtful interpretation of the Scriptures but the love of Jesus. Let us remember that he entered Samaria and sought out a woman scorned by her community, sometimes dined with prostitutes and tax collectors, and in the presence of a murderous crowd offered forgiveness to an adulteress. Being obedient to Jesus and following him faithfully will be just that gracious and just that risky.

COMPARING AND CONTRASTING
SOME DISTINGUISHING WESLEYAN AND FUNDAMENTALIST EXPRESSIONS OF THE CHRISTIAN FAITH

H. Ray Dunning, PhD

■ Have you ever attempted to fit a square peg into a round hole? Try as we might, eventually we must admit the object simply does not fit. The same is true in theology. There are some doctrines held by some parts of the Christian church that simply will not fit into the doctrinal framework of other theological traditions. Sooner or later we have to recognize the incompatibility. For example, we cannot take the belief that from eternity God elected some people to salvation and some to eternal damnation and fit it into a theological system that believes Christ died for the salvation of all persons. The one conviction will not fit into the other.

Similarly, some primary convictions that characterize fundamentalism cannot be incorporated into Wesleyan theology without seriously distorting the latter. The "fit" would be forced and counterproductive. This chapter examines some distinguishing doctrines of both fundamentalism and Wesleyanism and explains why, in spite of important similarities, they are incompatible in important respects. This requires comparison and contrast.

Challenges Ahead

Comparing and contrasting how different parts of Christ's church understand the Christian faith is difficult, partly because theological perspectives go through transitions. Consequently, identifying a doctrinal position runs the risk of being dated and hence at least partly misrepresentative. In the words of Anglican New Testament scholar N. T. Wright, "Reality isn't what it used to be."[1]

One reason for transitions in doctrinal families is that context has much to do with how Christian doctrine is understood and stated. For example, we can trace how the historical and social contexts of Martin Luther or John Calvin or John Wesley affected their perceptions of Christian doctrine, the church, and the world. The same is true for us. So we should refrain from easily equating how we understand a doctrine or a doctrinal tradition with how someone in an earlier era and culture understood it.

The rule applies to both fundamentalism and Wesleyan theology, each of which has undergone important transitions.[2] For example, changes in Methodism happened when it was transplanted to the American colonies. There were even significant differences among Methodists in England; Wesley was not a Calvinist, but there was a Calvinistic branch of Methodists. The American Holiness Movement of the late nineteenth and early twentieth centuries, now represented by the Church of the Nazarene, the Wesleyan Church, and the Free Methodist Church among others, diverged from John Wesley to some extent, even though advocates of the Holiness Movement insisted on their fidelity to Wesley. More recently, theologians in the Holiness Movement have sought to become more faithful to Wesley than were some of their holiness forebears. In the course of its history, the Holiness Movement has been significantly impacted by fundamentalism, and that has affected its fidelity to Wesleyan theology.[3] This mixed picture prompted historian George M. Marsden to identify the Holiness Movement as one part of fundamentalism.[4]

Comparing and contrasting the eighteenth-century theology of John Wesley with early twentieth-century fundamentalism requires that we proceed carefully. Fundamentalism in the twentieth century engaged in a controversy with a modernist form of theology John Wesley never encountered. That difference affected how each understood and articulated the Christian faith, and it affects any comparison and contrast of the two. Fundamentalism faced opponents not on Wesley's radar screen. Ignoring such differences leaves the two traditions often "speaking past each other."

Another challenge associated with comparing and contrasting theological traditions and trying to make honest appraisals of each is the temptation to construct straw men. Straw men are simplistic misrepresentations of another's position; they can be easily demolished. Each doctrinal tradition must be fairly presented by its critics. Christian charity and hope for real dialogue require this. Some contemporary fundamentalists, for example, insist that accusing fundamentalism of teaching that the very words of the Bible were dictated by God is unfair. They say no informed fundamentalist ever taught that writers of the Bible were little more than human typewriters on which the Holy Spirit wrote the biblical text.

Thinking of fundamentalism as a monolithic movement is an error. Ernest R. Sandeen, one of the two most significant historians of fundamentalism, observed, there "seems to be no unity" among those who identify themselves as fundamentalists.[5] A distinction must be made between "evangelical" scholars who represent historic fundamentalism and "folk fundamentalists."[6] The first group rejects the narrowness that characterized much of early fundamentalism. Much of what they teach agrees with authentic Wesleyan theology.[7] The second group perpetuates some of the more objectionable features of fundamentalism.

A similar observation must be made of the Wesleyan tradition. As with fundamentalism, there are among Wesleyans those who hold to diverse interpretations of certain beliefs about Christian experience and doctrine. As noted below, some of this results from various features of fundamentalism infiltrating the Holiness Movement.

Comparisons and Contrasts

Before comparing and contrasting specific theological differences between fundamentalism and the Wesleyan tradition, we will profit from noting the central perspective or orientation of each tradition. Theological systems that are internally coherent, that is, not self-contradictory or merely eclectic, contain a "control belief" or unifying principle that gives them consistency. The control beliefs of fundamentalism and Wesleyan theology are identifiable.

The fundamentalist control belief and starting point is truth, understood in a particular way. It is known as the correspondence theory of truth. Truth, according to this view, is the *characteristic of a proposition* that corresponds with external reality and events. The philosophical assumption behind this interpretation is a philosophy known as Scottish realism, or common-sense philosophy. It assumes that the human mind, through the various senses, has a direct, immediate, and accurate apprehension of objects in the external world. By implication, this knowledge provides an adequate understanding of the meaning and significance of the observable external world. For example, to question the adequacy of one's immediate perceptions of a desk is for the average person to fly in the face of common sense. Thus, the designation of this philosophy: common-sense philosophy.

Commitment to the correspondence theory of truth and common-sense philosophy helps explain why fundamentalist theologians are keenly interested in apologetics (giving a reasoned account of Christian faith). They believe they can and must convincingly demonstrate through reason and historical evidence the accuracy of all events reported in the Bible. This would include events as diverse as the story of Abraham and the resurrection of Jesus.

The fundamentalist understanding of truth (objective and demonstrable facts) contrasts sharply with the Wesleyan understanding of truth. John Wesley, who lived during a time when rational apologetics were rampant, questioned the adequacy of the traditional arguments for God's existence. He explicitly denied that reason alone can conclusively prove this—or any other—theological claim.[8]

The approach to apologetics Wesley would support is seen in Jesus' prayer for his disciples (John 17). He prayed for their unity "that the world may believe that thou hast sent me" (v. 21, KJV). Unity of the Spirit in love in Christ's church, not rational argument, will be the primary authentication that the Father sent his Son. Also, 1 Peter's emphasis on the holy life as following "in [the] steps" of Christ makes the same point (2:21). His admonition is, "Always be ready to make your defense to anyone who demands from you an accounting for the hope that is in you" (3:15). In context, Peter's instruction refers to how Christians must live, not to doctrinal belief and argument.

The fundamentalist confidence in reason's ability to demonstrate the truth of the Bible is reflected in fundamentalism's understanding of faith. Instead of faith being viewed as a personal relation with God based on trust, it is seen as belief in or assent to true statements or propositions about God. Christian faith becomes primarily assent to infallible biblical propositions. This must be balanced by the fact that fundamentalist piety stresses faith in Jesus Christ for salvation and the importance of Christian piety. At the practical level Wesleyans share with fundamentalists a commitment to discipleship. But at the academic level, among fundamentalist apologists or spokespersons the difference becomes much sharper. James Barr notes that "faith is betrayed by the fundamentalist apparatus of argument. For faith it substitutes dependence on rational use of evidence; and in place of the religious functioning of the Bible it takes, as primary guarantee of the authority of scripture, the absence of error, especially in its historical details."[9]

We have seen that truth is the control belief for fundamentalism and have seen how that affects the fundamentalist understanding of faith. In sharp contrast, salvation is the control belief for Wesleyan theology. Its approach to Scripture is reflected in Jesus' critique of the Pharisees who searched the Scriptures thinking they could provide eternal life. Jesus corrected the Pharisees by saying, "The scriptures testify of me" (John 5:39, paraphrase). So Jesus the Redeemer, salvation, not the Bible as the depository of truth, constitutes the control belief for Wesleyans. John Wesley compared the process of salvation to a house. Prevenient grace is described as the *porch*, justification as the *door*, and sanctification or holiness as the *rooms* of the house, together encompassing the whole process of salvation in this life.

This should not be taken to mean that Wesleyan theology is unconcerned about truth but that Wesley's understanding of truth is biblical and Christological rather than philosophical and propositional. In the Bible, truth (*emet*, Hebrew) refers to God's faithfulness to his word, particularly his promises of salvation. This understanding informs George Eldon Ladd's exposition of John 8:32: "'To know the truth' means to know God's saving purpose as it is embodied in Christ."[10] This understanding of the Bible's truth allows Wesleyans to recognize that although there may be minor errors in the text, God has been faithfully using the Bible for centuries to bring lost human beings into a saving relation with himself.

With these contrasting control beliefs in mind we can now examine two significant comparisons and contrasts between Wesleyan theology and fundamentalism.

First, both Wesleyan theology and fundamentalism are committed to the authority of Scripture. But the two traditions differ significantly over how the Bible's authority should be understood. Generally, fundamentalists insist on the inerrancy of the biblical text. The objective inerrancy marking the Bible is its source of authority. The Princeton theologians—a group of scholars connected with Princeton Theological Seminary during the modernist controversy—fathered this position. They said inerrancy should be attributed only to the original autographs of the books. However, the original autographs no longer exist. So it is impossible to verify the fundamentalist claim about absolute inerrancy. Even though most fundamentalists are Calvinistic in their theology, this position departs from Calvin's own teaching.[11]

Parts of the Wesleyan tradition have allowed their emotional ties with the aims of fundamentalism to saddle them with a fundamentalist doctrine of Scripture.[12] But in fact, the fundamentalist position on inerrancy is primarily at odds with Wesleyan theology. Unlike fundamentalism, Wesleyan theology teaches that the Bible's authority is validated by the internal witness of the Holy Spirit. No amount of external authority and argument, no matter how intellectually impressive, can compel adherence to the Scriptures or disclose their real meaning. This can come only from an internal conviction born of the Holy Spirit.[13] This position was stated by twentieth-century Wesleyan theologian H. Orton Wiley. He rejected the fundamentalist effort to defend the Bible's authority on the basis of the written text: "Spiritual men and women—those filled with the Holy Spirit . . . do not rest merely in the letter [of scripture] which must be defended by argument. They have a broader and more substantial basis for their faith. It rests in their risen Lord, the glorified Christ."[14]

Wiley is showing fidelity to John Wesley, whose defining interest in the Bible was its unerring story of salvation, of the Redeemer God, not in its detailed inerrancy. Wesley's passion was a faithful response to the biblical call to faith in Jesus Christ, to confessing him as Lord of the church and the world, to deliverance from sin, and to assurance of acceptance by God through Christ. It is thoroughly Wesleyan to affirm the infallibility of Scripture if that means infallibly "revealing the will of God . . . in all things necessary to our salvation."[15] The truth of the Bible refers to God's faithfulness to his promises, particularly his promise of salvation.

New Testament scholar N. T. Wright has accurately expressed Wesleyan theology's position:

> God's authority vested in scripture is designed, as all God's authority is designed, to liberate human beings, to judge and condemn evil and sin in the world in order to set people free to be fully human. That's what God is in the business of doing. That is what his authority is there *for*. And when we use a shorthand phrase like "authority of scripture" that is what we ought to be meaning. It is an authority with this shape and character, this purpose and goal.[16]

Second, in addition to Scripture, Wesleyan theology employs subsidiary sources for understanding and expressing the Christian faith. They are often referred to as the Wesleyan quadrilateral. In addition to Scripture, the quadrilateral includes *tradition, reason,* and *experience,* which always serve Scripture in subordinate roles. *Tradition* refers to "the church's time-honored practices of worship, service, and critical reflection."[17] It includes the ancient ecumenical creeds and their definitions of Christian faith, the writings of individual theologians who have been widely accepted as teachers of the church (e.g., Augustine, Thomas Aquinas, Martin Luther, John Calvin, and John Wesley), and the confessions and articles of faith of particular denominations. *Reason* refers to knowledge of the world gained through systematic reflection and scientific investigation. Reason in the service of faith also includes weighing the meaning of a biblical text and historical study of the Bible (e.g., its cultural contexts and process of composition and development). *Experience* includes the religious experience of individuals as monitored by the corporate experience of the church. Individual religious experience must be governed by the Bible and validated by the wider experience of the body of Christ. New Testament scholar Richard B. Hays, reflecting the spirit of the Wesleyan quadrilateral, says, "Experience serves not only to illuminate the meaning of [a biblical] text but also to confirm the testimony of scripture in the hearts and lives of the community." This is the internal witness of the Holy Spirit (*testimonium internum Spiritus Sancti*). It is "what John Wesley meant when he spoke of 'experimental religion': experience is the living appropriation of the text, which becomes self-attesting as it is experienced in faith."[18]

Tradition and reason, then, serve as resources for properly interpreting Scripture. Experience is a confirming source. John Wesley repeatedly tested the correctness of his interpretation of Scripture as it relates to Christian discipleship against experience itself. Does the interpretation practically play out in Christian life? In response to this question, from time to time Wesley found it necessary to adjust how he understood Scripture.

The same test is used by contemporary Wesleyans. For example, how Christian holiness is understood must be tested against its adequacy for actual Christian life today.[19] Consequently, for Wesleyan theology, tradition can be revised if it is discovered that it isn't supported by sound biblical examination and corporate Christian experience. Tradition, reason, and experience all doggedly stand under Scripture's authority.

Here we observe a major contrast between fundamentalism and Wesleyan theology. In spite of fundamentalism's supposed high doctrine of Scripture, it actually forces Scripture to bow to tradition. This charge was made by James Barr. He supported his charge by showing how fundamentalists defend the Mosaic authorship of all the Pentateuch (the first five books of the Old Testament) in opposition to believing that various literary sources came together to compose the Pentateuch (known as the documentary hypothesis). Barr correctly observes that only the fundamentalist insistence on single Mosaic authorship, not the Pentateuch itself, requires rejection of multiple sources. Tradition takes precedence over Scripture, over what the text clearly indicates—or does not indicate—about itself.

Unlike the latitude provided by the Wesleyan quadrilateral, fundamentalist bondage to tradition carries harmful implications for biblical interpretation. It seems to require a slavish adherence to the literal meaning of every passage without regard for historical or cultural context. Bondage to tradition requires an unnecessary struggle to reconcile passages that are apparently contradictory. How extensively this plays out in actual practice is open to examination.

But clearly the Wesleyan quadrilateral makes no such demands upon biblical interpretation and the Bible's history. John Wesley, who was completely dedicated to the truth of Scripture, relied upon what he called "the whole tenor of scripture," or occasionally the "analogy of faith." This, it seems, is what is today called biblical theology. In Wesley's words, biblical theology identifies and relies upon the "whole tenor of scripture." That is, it examines the theology that comes to expression by letting the text speak for itself, not by imposing a prior theology or worldview or tradition upon it. This approach, so consistent with Wesley, treats diverse passages and permits them, in their own way, to express their theological content.

A particular example of how the Wesleyan approach to Scripture plays out in practice will be instructive. Instead of trying to justify God's call of females into ordained Christian ministry by a torturous interpretation of 1 Cor. 14:33b-35, Wesleyan scholars reply on the basis of the "whole tenor of scripture," which reveals the elimination of gender privilege in the gospel of Jesus Christ.

Conclusion

Fundamentalists and Wesleyans are sisters and brothers in Christ, members of the one holy, catholic, and apostolic church. A divisive spirit in Christ's

church is contrary to Wesleyan theology. At the same time, Wesleyans hold to some distinguishing doctrines they believe faithfully represent the Christian faith. These are convictions we have no desire to set aside; they cannot be easily accommodated to all other theological families. Denominations that adhere to a Wesleyan vision of the Christian faith have a right and a responsibility to insist that those who join their fellowship understand and adopt their primary convictions. New members cannot in good faith simply set Wesleyan theology aside in favor of other theological traditions. More pointedly, Wesleyan theology and fundamentalism cannot be successfully mixed.

WHY IT MATTERS
(Chapter 4)

Dwight Gunter, DMin, and Nina Gunter, DD

We were sitting in the family room listening to our son/grandson play a guitar his grandfather had given him—a 1946 Gibson. The sound was sweet, lyrical, and reflective. It occurred to us that the reason music could be made was because of tension between two points on a guitar string.

Therein lies a major difference between Wesleyan theology and fundamentalism, as Dr. Dunning has explained. Fundamentalism seeks to remove all intellectual tension, dismiss all questions about science that don't fit the fundamentalist scheme, and solve all problems associated with biblical scholarship. But Wesleyan theology makes music amid all these tensions without trying to dismiss them. It can live with the dissonance of paradox and with life's unanswerable questions.

Why does it matter? What difference does the distinction between fundamentalism and Wesleyan theology make in Christian faith and practice?

According to the laypersons who discussed chapter 4, the difference matters because "it is extremely important that clergy and laity truly understand our theology. We believe that doctrine informs action." And our actions reflect our beliefs. If you want to know what someone believes, they said, look at what they do instead of just listening to what they say. What Wesleyan theology teaches differs considerably from what fundamentalism teaches, and so do some of the actions that follow. Therefore, we should choose carefully and then put Wesleyan theology to work in how we interface with modern culture, including modern science. *It matters.*

If most modern persons were forced to choose between the absolutes of fundamentalism about history and science on the one hand, and modern science and historical re-search on the other, they would probably choose the latter. They know life is more complex than fundamentalism makes it out to be. Wesleyan theology doesn't require persons to make that choice. It teaches Christians how to hold fast to orthodox Christian faith while coming to grips with modernity. Fundamentalism is unnecessarily narrow and restrictive. Wesleyan theology points the way to intellectual honesty while holding fast to essential Christian doctrines. Fundamentalism is sharply black-and-white. Wesleyan theology is multifaceted and liberating. *The differences matter.*

Responding to Dr. Dunning, the lay participants speak again: "We are dealing with a topic that has major implications for how our Christian faith will be lived out in the world. Only if our doctrinal foundations are solid, will our expressions of faith be solid." *It matters.*

Furthermore, "Wesleyan theology and fundamentalism can't just co-exist without conflict." The differences are too great. Ignoring the differences has often led to confusion in Wesleyan denominations. Clergy and laypersons who adhere to Wesleyan theology often have their orthodoxy called into question by fundamentalists who believe Wesleyans ought to be fundamentalists. Although fundamentalism is seriously at odds with Wesleyan theology, it claims the high ground against those who disagree. A large part of the problem is that too many people who call themselves Wesleyan don't really understand the Wesleyan perspective on Christian faith and practice. *It matters.*

For Wesleyan theology the truth of the Christian faith is principally manifest in transformed lives characterized by love for God and neighbor. For fundamentalism the truth of the Christian faith is primarily a matter of factual claims supported by rational argumentation and the Bible. *The difference matters.*

Why does all this matter? Because where we invest our energies and direct our focus as Christians will have much to do with the form of our discipleship and the character of our Christian witness. Fundamentalism seems to emphasize proving and defending the Bible's inerrancy in all things and showing how wrong much of modern science is. Wesleyans, on the other hand, emphasize asking how the Scriptures teach them to live godly and responsible lives in the church and in the world. Principally they want to know how to announce God's grace to all. *Yes, it matters.*

There is an optimism in Wesleyan theology about God's grace as it relates to the salvation of all persons, honest scholarship, and the practice of good science—a radical optimism of grace. *It matters.*

There we sat, carried away by the music flowing from tension on the strings. The chords were beautiful, the dissonance intriguing, and the melodies and themes inspiring. Music!

Yes, if there is to be music in Christian faith and witness, Wesleyan theology matters.

FUNDAMENTALISM
AND SAUL'S ARMOR
Al Truesdale, PhD

■ One of our most familiar Bible stories is about David and Goliath. Israel's army was being intimidated by Goliath, a Philistine giant. Then a young shepherd boy who was delivering food to his brothers showed up. David rushed to the battle line to get a good look. He was dismayed to see that a mere Philistine had paralyzed the Lord's army. He quickly volunteered to fight Goliath. David believed the God who had saved him from a lion and a bear would give him victory over Goliath.

Wanting David to succeed, Saul began to prepare David for battle by dressing him in his own armor. But once outfitted, David became immobilized! Under its weight, he stumbled clumsily about. Saul's armor was impressive by military standards. But for God's purposes it was inferior. David's story has been a lesson to the faithful through the ages: "Do not try to fight in Saul's armor." Do not try to do the Lord's work with instruments inconsistent with his character and will.

During the late nineteenth and early twentieth centuries, evangelical Christians faced another "Goliath." They referred to it as liberalism or modernism. Certain historic doctrines of the Christian faith were under attack. Fundamentalism was one response to this Goliath.

"Fundamentalism," as observed in chapter 1, is a term derived from a series of publications titled

The Fundamentals: A Testimony to the Truth.[1] By the 1920s fundamentalists found themselves confronting a world that was embracing a secularity
unlike anything Christians had previously encountered. Questions about
the world and human meaning—traditionally answered by some version
of the Christian faith—were increasingly being answered in academia and
the public square with no reference to God.[2] Evangelical Protestants, who
represented much of what had been America's dominant spiritual voice,
watched the curtains rise on "the profound spiritual and cultural crisis of
the twentieth century,"[3] the result of what Charles Taylor calls "an expanding universe of unbelief." The West was moving "from being a society where
it was virtually impossible not to believe in God, to one in which belief is
optional, often frowned upon."[4]

A rising tide of biblical criticism coming from Europe was questioning many traditional views of the Bible and sometimes challenging
historic Christian doctrines. The challenges included questioning the deity of Christ and his atonement, divine revelation, and in some instances
whether Jesus was even a real historical figure. An evolutionary model
was often applied to all religions and scriptures, including Christianity
and the Bible. The Old Testament record supposedly revealed evolution
from a crude, even polytheistic, religion to a more sophisticated one that
advocated one God—Yahweh. It was common to make a distinction between the "religion of Jesus" and the "religion about Jesus" that, according
to many critics, unjustifiably turned a Jewish moral prophet into a deity.

Fundamentalism was a "genuine religious movement"[5] that arose
from a legitimate desire to defend the Christian faith against its modern
critics inside and outside the church. That part is commendable. But we
raise a question: Were the methods chosen consistent with the faith itself
and with the Scriptures themselves? Or were they a ver-
sion of "fighting in Saul's armor"?

The most sophisticated theology employed in
defense of some aspects of fundamentalism came
from a group of scholars connected with Princeton

Theological Seminary. They developed what came to be known as Princeton theology. The Princeton theologians were not themselves fundamentalists in the strict sense of the term.[6] Unfortunately they chose to use misleading and counterproductive weapons in defense of the Christian faith. They sought to make the Christian faith stronger but succeeded in making it weaker. Their efforts to defend the Bible against modern criticism transformed it into something the Bible was not meant to be.

Princeton theology provided much of the theological and intellectual fuel for fundamentalism. It was fathered by Princeton's founding professor and staunch Calvinist, Archibald Alexander (1772–1851), a proponent of Scottish common-sense philosophy (explained below). Charles Hodge, a voluminous writer in defense of orthodoxy, was Alexander's most famous student.[7] He was succeeded by his son, Archibald Alexander Hodge (1823-86), who in turn was succeeded by Benjamin B. Warfield (1851–1921). Princeton theology achieved its most notable defense in the work of J. Gresham Machen (1881–1937), professor of New Testament and a prominent Presbyterian minister. By Machen's estimate, Princeton theology equaled Christian theology.[8]

No matter how we evaluate the fundamentalist responses to modernity, the perceived threats they battled were not phantoms. Nevertheless, we must evaluate *how* and *how well* they responded. Doing so will be instructive for us today.

Some ways of responding to threats to the Christian faith are better than others. The nature of the faith should decide. Otherwise, we risk misrepresenting it and even changing its meaning. For example, how would Christianity have changed had early Christians rioted and pillaged in response to persecution?

Fundamentalism, inspired by the Princeton theologians, erred by choosing to wear two pieces of "Saul's armor" in defense of Christian doctrine: (1) the philosophy of Scottish realism and (2) natural science as shaped by Sir Francis Bacon[9] and Sir Isaac Newton.

These instruments shaped the fundamentalist understanding of revelation, the nature of biblical authority, and the doctrines contained therein. The models they chose led to identifying Christian revelation as resting upon observable and provable facts[10] and as universally accessible through the right use of reason. The Princeton theologians and fundamentalists were confident the two instruments would provide (1) rationally binding support for the Scriptures and Christian doctrine, (2) certainty that God is the Creator, and (3) a sure defense against Christianity's modern critics. The confidence proved erroneous.

Making God and the Bible "Reasonable"

Scottish realism, common-sense philosophy, or "theistic common sense," as historian Mark A. Noll prefers,[11] taught that all knowledge begins with self-evident truths—facts—we cannot avoid believing (e.g., the physical world is real, and there is a difference between right and wrong). It claimed to see facts precisely, whether facts about God, the Bible, human nature, morality, or the natural world. Following the inductive method of Francis Bacon (1561–1626), philosophy and science should build upon self-evident truths.

Scottish common sense gave birth to a moral philosophy that, as Mark Noll shows, departed significantly from the theological grounding of morality as insisted upon by the Reformers (John Wesley included). It was replaced by an innate and universal "moral sense." Noll quotes Norman Fiering: "The guiding assumption behind almost all of the new work was the belief that God's intentions for man, His expectations of human beings as moral creatures, could be discovered independently of the traditional sources of religious authority, through a close investigation of human nature."[12] As important as this development is, our interest in common-sense philosophy leads in a different direction. But it is important to note the appeal to a form of reason not fundamentally dependent upon divine revelation and new creation through the Holy

Spirit. The appeal shows up in Princeton theology's doctrine of biblical authority.

The most creative period of common-sense philosophy spans the work of Scottish philosophers and Presbyterian ministers Francis Hutcheson (1694–1747) and Thomas Reid (1710-96). Reid would provide the definitive statement of Scottish common-sense philosophy. Hutcheson's moral philosophy gained traction in influential American colleges by the 1750s. The Reverend John Witherspoon (1723-94), a well-known Scottish minister, spurred a broad acceptance of common-sense philosophy in America after becoming president of Princeton in 1768.[13] Largely through his influence, common-sense philosophy became the dominant philosophy in American academic institutions. It seemed to offer a firm foundation for a scientific approach to all reality, including God. Its dominance continued into the nineteenth century.

Common sense was a democratic philosophy because it did not move very far from popular views about the nature of the material world, the soul, and God. Given by God, common sense is a dependable guide to truth for all persons. The mind is so constructed that it can directly know certain things, for example, cause and effect, which proves for all to see that only God can account for the design we observe in creation.[14] By relying upon the direct testimony of consciousness—to "self-evident truths" or "intuitive truths"—common-sense philosophy claimed to resolve the doubts other philosophies created.[15] On this basis, common sense developed unassailable principles for settling all disputed opinions. It built a comprehensive and understandable intellectual structure that gave access to the world as it really is. If a person will just observe and think correctly—believe propositions that are so evident to the intellect that one cannot justifiably fail to believe them—he or she will not only learn about the world but also inevitably see that God exists, just as the Bible says. Stated more strongly, "unprejudiced" common sense provides validation for the Bible and Christianity.[16]

One of the most important things common sense supposedly permits us to know is that God could not and would not convey his inerrant divine truth through an errant source or document. Hence, in the Bible God has given an inerrant source of truth. Based on this assumption, the Princeton theologians produced a systematic defense of an inerrant Bible and a literalist method of interpretation. Either the whole Bible must be inerrant or the Scriptures as a whole must be false.[17] Inerrancy applies to all the Bible's affirmations, including physical and historical data.

In this light, assuming the Baconian method of induction, the Princeton theologians insisted theology is a science. Charles Hodge claimed, "If natural science be concerned with the facts and laws of nature, theology is concerned with the facts and the principles of the Bible." Just as natural science systematizes facts of nature and ascertains the laws that determine them, the task of theology "is to systematize the facts of the Bible, and ascertain the principles or general truths which those facts involve."[18] Nancy T. Ammerman describes the product as a "systematic, rational approach to finding and organizing the facts of Scripture." It "reflects the nineteenth century scientific world from which [fundamentalism] emerged."[19]

Not surprisingly, the Bible came to be seen by the Princeton theologians and those who followed them as a treasury of objective facts about things divine, historical, and physical. The facts could be mined and systematized into objective, timeless, universal truth. Given the common-sense confidence that God structured the human mind so as to access truth, the systematized truths of the Bible would be available to anyone willing to use common sense properly. George M. Marsden observes that "intellectually the believer and the non-believer stood on common ground."[20] Truth, including religious truth, became largely identified with "fact."

What constitutes Scripture's authority? The Princeton theologians answered: the Bible's authority resides *in itself*, in the text. The entire Bible is inspired. The text constitutes a verifiable theological science that exhibits and confirms its inspiration.[21] And the inspiration of the Scriptures can be proven through the use of common sense, beginning with the self-evident truth that an infallible God speaks through an infallible and confirmable witness. Not all biblical teachings are equally clear, explicit, and important, but the trustworthiness of the biblical writers confirms all doctrines.

Accordingly, the Bible needs no authenticating witness beyond itself. Its authority is wholly objective (in the text) and empirically verifiable. Any further confirmation would undercut its own perfection. Historian of fundamentalism Ernest Sandeen observes, "The witness of the Spirit, though not overlooked, cannot be said to play any important role in Princeton thought."[22] How unlike John Wesley, who believed "the Spirit of God not only once inspired those who wrote [the Scriptures], but continually inspires, supernaturally assists those that read it with earnest prayer."[23]

Observe also that biblical authority is primarily a matter of knowledge, of reason, of facts. In good "scientific" form, confirmation of the Bible's authority results from a compounding accumulation of evidence provided by factual data. Inspiration extends to every book and every word. Even a single proved error would dismantle the Bible's inerrancy.

For many Christians today, all this makes perfect sense and there is no good reason to question it. However, what we have described is potentially very injurious to the Christian faith.

Let's consider some of the problems. The Princeton theologians believed they were defending classical Protestant doctrine, but they were not. By treating the Scriptures as divine data analogous to the data scientists examine, the Princeton theologians and their fundamentalist followers seriously departed from the Protestant Reformation. By lodging inspiration in the text and entrusting the Bible's authority to a total absence of error, they walked away from the Reformers. They did what the

Reformers refused to do and thereby altered the nature of the Bible. Their error was twofold.

First, they badly misidentified and misplaced the *source* of biblical authority and inspiration. Anglican scholar Philip Edgcumbe Hughes says the Reformers repeatedly emphasized that "it is only through the grace of the internal operation of the Holy Spirit in heart and mind that the message of Scripture can be understood and appropriated."[24] The Holy Spirit, not the Bible itself, is the locus of the Bible's inspiration and authority.

When rebuking Erasmus for failing to support the clarity of the Scriptures, Martin Luther said, "Nobody who has not the Spirit of God sees a jot of what is in the Scriptures." Even if people can "discuss and quote all that is in the Scripture, they do not understand or really know any of it" apart from "the knowledge of the heart" the Holy Spirit makes possible. The Spirit is necessary for understanding "every part of Scripture."[25]

No one affirmed this more clearly than the Reformer John Calvin (1509-64). He placed the authority and instruction of the Scriptures above the authority of the church and its traditions.[26] Responding to those who use reason to refute the testimony of the Bible, Calvin says, "The testimony of the Spirit is superior to reason. For as God alone can properly bear witness to his own words, so these words will not obtain full credit in the hearts of men, until they are sealed by the inward testimony of the Spirit [*testimonium Spiritus Sancti*]."[27]

Calvin discusses many features of the Bible by which its dignity and majesty are demonstrated "to the pious." True, our "heavenly Father manifests his presence" there. But none of this is simply accessible to rational proof; it is revealed to faith alone. "Scripture suffices to give a saving knowledge of God [only] when its certainty is founded on the inward persuasion of the Holy Spirit."[28] Knowledge of the Bible's real meaning and authority are inseparable from the grace of regeneration.

What about John Wesley (1703-91), who could say, "Oh, give me that book! At any price give me the book of God"?[29] Wesleyan scholar Randy Maddox indicates that though Wesley did not have a well-developed doctrine of the internal witness of the Holy Spirit, he nevertheless believed that for the Scriptures to communicate God's truth to us, to have their proper impact, the Holy Spirit must open our spiritual senses so that we can perceive and attest to the truth to which they bear witness. Wesley affirmed God's guidance of Scripture's authors. But embracing its saving truth comes not through standard rational processes or empirical evidence.[30] It happens as a gracious gift of the Holy Spirit, a gift that must be constantly renewed through reliance upon the Spirit.[31] "We need the same Spirit to *understand* the Scripture which enabled the holy men of old to *write* it."[32]

Wesley defended the role of reason in service to the Christian faith. But he understood reason as "faith seeking understanding." Methodist theologian William Ragsdale Cannon (1916-97) says Wesley and the Methodists did not try to defend Christianity by using rational systems. The surest way to lead persons to evangelical faith, they believed, was by a "positive affirmation of the principles of the Bible in character and life."[33]

Luther, Calvin, and Wesley were being obedient to what the apostle Paul says in 1 Cor. 2:6-14. He explains the irreplaceable role of the Holy Spirit in revelation. Persons who are "unspiritual" cannot receive the gifts of God; for them the things of God are "foolishness" (v. 14). The gifts of God can only be "spiritually discerned" (v. 14).

Judged by these standards, the Princeton theologians and their followers erred grievously. John Calvin explicitly cut off the peg on which the Princetonians hung their hats. By embracing the modernist confidence in reason, they forgot that knowing the Bible as God's Word is principally a matter of soteriology (salvation), not "theological science," argumentative reason, and empirical facts.[34] Calvin could have taught them that it is quite insufficient for the mind to be convinced unless "the heart [is also] strengthened and supported by the Spirit's power."[35] The Bible's authority resides in the miracle of transformation wrought by the Holy Spirit. "Then only does Scripture suffice to give a saving knowledge of God."[36]

Second, by viewing the Bible as a storehouse of inerrant objective facts about things divine, the Princeton theologians closed the Bible to all but a surface treatment of its history and literature. Ironically, a theology that claimed to take the Bible seriously actually did the opposite. Princeton theology and fundamentalism cannot take seriously the Bible's own internal history and complexity. Nor can they tolerate the many twists and turns by which the Old and New Testament canons achieved their present form. For example, features of the book of Jonah strongly suggest it was written after the Jews began returning from Babylonian exile in 538 BC, not while Nineveh was still the capital of mighty Assyria. Jonah may have been written to oppose religious introversion among the returning exiles. But the book has Jonah in Nineveh *before* its destruction in 612 BC. If we adhere to what the Princeton theologians said about the Bible's factual inerrancy, further questions about Jonah's date, context, and most importantly its message will be off limits. Placing the book *after* the exile would challenge the inerrant "truth" of the Bible. Charles Hodge said the Bible's inspiration "extends to [its] words."[37]

Ironically, fundamentalism forces the Bible to remain silent about itself, namely, about its own history. The Princeton theologians wanted to make the Bible richer and stronger. But their doctrine of biblical authority and inerrancy actually made it poorer and weaker. What the Princeton theologians imposed upon the Bible, the Bible doesn't require of itself.

By contrast, Luther, Calvin, and Wesley believed the "infallibility" of the Bible is that it faithfully leads us to the Redeemer. Its inerrancy resides in its unfailing testimony to the triune God.

Let us not fail to notice that the riveting interest New Testament authors have in the Old Testament is that it anticipates Christ the Redeemer. "Beginning at Moses and all the prophets, [Jesus] expounded unto them in all the scriptures the things concerning himself" (Luke 24:27, KJV).

Science: A Sure Public Path to God?

Influenced by Scottish realism, those who formed the ranks of fundamentalism believed English philosopher and scientist Francis Bacon (1561–1626) had provided a surefire method for building upon the foundations of common sense. Bacon is remembered as one of the fathers of the scientific method. He spelled this out in the *Novum Organum* (1620), the new organ or method for investigating the natural world. With his logic of induction, Bacon revolutionized the path to knowledge of the world: (1) examine the particulars; (2) test and build on pieces of confirmed knowledge; and (3) build toward more general or universal causes and forms. Only what is achieved in this way can be properly claimed as knowledge. Whether in theology or physics, morality or biology, the Princeton theologians believed, careful observers need only proceed by induction to confirm and classify the certainties common sense supports. Fact upon observed fact, truth upon truth, leads to certainty.

The process supposedly delivers certainty that the world was created and is governed by an all-wise, benevolent God. He administers his creation by a system of laws rational persons can amply discern. If uncertainty remains, it is because we have not carefully examined the data.

Theologians who cast their lot with this method saw natural science as objective (lacking in any subjective bias), unified (whether the parts be biology, physics, or the truths of Christianity), cumulative, and discoverable in the "forum of pure reason."[38] Natural science and Christian theology, it was believed, form "an impregnable synthesis between faith and science."[39]

Speaking that way may seem strange today. But remember, Warfield and his successors were devotees of the Enlightenment's confidence in reason as expressed in Scottish realism. Newtonian science with its knowable and invariable laws, not the later relativity of Einstein, provided their understanding of natural science.

In the late nineteenth century, George Marsden observes, evangelicals were in principle "deeply wedded to a scientific culture, so long as it left room (indeed a privileged place of honor) [for] their version of Christianity."[40] Science was a trusted ally of Christian truth. God's revelation in the laws of nature supports God's revelation attested in the Bible and Christian doctrine.

There is one unified science, one unified reason, and one unified conclusion whether in science or theology. Natural science and theology advance along the same path—provable facts—and both arrive at the same goal: certainty. Since there is only one universal truth—God's unified and accessible truth—science itself, when properly pursued, will confirm the principal Christian convictions about God, humans, and the world.

A challenge to this apparently permanent alliance had been building since the eighteenth-century Enlightenment. It increased in the nineteenth century and matured in the twentieth century. Challenges came from many quarters: Immanuel Kant in philosophy, Auguste Comte and Emile Durkheim in sociology, Wellhausen and Graf in German biblical criticism, Sigmund Freud in psychology, and Charles Darwin in biology. What became increasingly clear to many orthodox Christians was that the alliance between Baconian science and religion had trapped fundamentalists into saying things and making claims that never should have been made. They realized the Bible simply did not make those claims for itself.

The Princeton theologians had confidently applied a scientific model to the Bible and had staked its truth on how well it succeeded. However, it was becoming increasingly clear to many that the kind of certainty and knowledge that interested post-Newtonian science is not the kind traditionally provided by common sense, the Princeton theologians, and

Newtonian science. The old alliance between science and theology was unraveling; science itself was changing.

Perhaps the major crisis in the traditional alliance resulted from the development of the Darwinian theory of evolution. Darwin undercut the confirmation for creation traditionally provided by common sense. He believed all species of life descended over time from a common ancestor through a process of natural selection (heritable variations in traits that maximize adaptability and hence survival), not by divine creation of each species as Genesis indicates and common sense supports. Given sufficient time, the complete diversity of living organisms on earth, past and present, can be explained through selection of this sort. Darwin's observations and conclusions were published in his *On the Origin of Species* (1859).

By the late 1870s many evangelicals had come to recognize that the explanatory power of Darwin's conclusions were too impressive to be dismissed.[41] Many thought Darwin and the Bible could be reconciled. Princeton theologian Charles Hodge was not one of them. In *What Is Darwinism?* (1848) Hodge answered, Darwinism is atheism. His indictment was unleashed because Darwin rejected any obvious role for divine purpose and direction in the evolutionary process. Instead of nature declaring God's glory as Creator, Darwin asserted that "from the war of nature, from famine and death, the most exalted object which we are capable of conceiving, namely, the production of the higher animals, directly follows. There is," Darwin said, "grandeur in this view of life." It is all too easy "to hide our ignorance" of the undirected evolutionary process "under such expressions as the 'plan of creation' [and] 'unity of design.'"[42]

The Princeton theologians and fundamentalists had cast their lot with common sense (Scottish realism), Bacon, and Newton. However, in the future Darwin and his successors[43] would set the ground rules for the conversation between science and Christian doctrine. Scientific research would not proceed along the lines of Scottish realism and the access it had given to theological and scientific certainty. Instead, science would build upon a new foundation.[44] In the end, Darwin said, evolutionary descent with modification will reveal "the origin of man and his history."[45]

The old order had dissolved, even if many refused to recognize it. As the sciences went their way, the fundamentalist investment became increasingly difficult to preserve. For fundamentalist leaders to this day it is impossible to admit that the truth and authority of the Bible and Christian faith might not be *of a kind* that matches the truth and authority that interests scientists. Undaunted, fundamentalists continue to claim either that science will support their observations about the world or that it just isn't good science.

Conclusion

A lamentable error lay at the root of the Princeton alliance between Christian doctrine and science. No matter how well intended, the Princeton theologians granted too much authority to reason and science for telling us what God is like and what the Bible is and means. By subjecting God to types of knowledge and research tailored for knowing the finite world, they effectively turned God into one more empirical or concrete knowable "thing" that could be examined and known as finite things are examined and known.

Theologian William Placher notes that instead of successfully combating modernity, fundamentalism actually submits to it by trying to make God fit into modernity's way of knowing and proving things. So ironically, fundamentalism is actually captured by what it supposedly opposes.[46] "If we try to talk about God in a way that fits God into human categories and systems, we end up not with God but with an idol"[47] who is not the free and sovereign triune God.

The book of Hebrews says that knowing God as the Creator comes principally not from the world but from faith, faith that has encountered the eternal God in radical transformation. "By faith we understand that the worlds were prepared by the word of God, so that what is seen was made from things that are not visible" (11:3). Colossians says the same. By faith we know that through Christ "all things in heaven and on earth were created, things visible and invisible" (1:16). All other "sources" are secondary and must be relied on as such.

Fundamentalism, with the best of intentions, departs from the certainty obtained through faith in the risen Lord and relocates certainty about the world's origin in the world itself. It does the same with the Bible by placing primary certainty about its authority in the Bible itself.

Those are errors we should not repeat.

WHY IT MATTERS

(Chapter 5)

Philip Hamner, MDiv, and Vicki Copp, DMin

Al Truesdale has urged us to pay attention to the historical roots of fundamentalism that led many evangelical Christians down a dangerous path. As he points out, the Christian faith was under enormous pressure during the nineteenth century. Cultural, intellectual, and philosophical pressures challenged Christians of that era to reevaluate the faith they so dearly loved. The mistake made by many was that they chose to wear "Saul's armor" in response to the challenges. Those who chose fundamentalism as their response tried to do the right thing—defend the Christian faith—in the wrong way. Unintentionally, in important ways they undermined the faith they wanted to defend. As Truesdale notes, "The Bible came to be seen by the Princeton theologians and those who followed them as a treasury of objective facts about things divine, historical, and physical."

That is the past. We are responsible for the church today. But we can learn from the past. Attempts to articulate the Christian faith in ways that don't adequately consider how the Holy Spirit leads the church will result in failure for doctrine and Christian witness. One failure involves viewing the Bible primarily as a revealed and authoritative record of divine truths and facts that must be believed. This badly misrepresents the Bible's purpose and the nature of biblical authority. It fails to recognize that Scripture's authority is something the Holy Spirit alone can establish. Fundamentalism turns the Bible into a body of divine information anyone who reasons properly can readily access. In its doctrine of Scripture, fundamentalism departs from historic Christian practice, certainly from the major Protestant Reformers.

There are times when our faith is confirmed by things that happen in our culture, such as when we see that prayer and a loving community really do result in people recovering from family tragedy or substance abuse. Or we see our Christian faith publically confirmed when the recidivism of prisoners who have benefitted from a faith-based ministry declines significantly. But there are other times when secular culture and models are directly at odds with Christian faith. Scripture tells us to expect this: "All who want to live a godly life in Christ Jesus will be persecuted" (2 Tim. 3:12). Being at odds with how an unbelieving world perceives the things of God is inherent in our faith. To expect those who have never been enlightened by the Holy Spirit to understand the truth of Scripture on their own, just because it is written, is erroneous. Knowing the truth and purpose of Scripture—that it can show the ways of God and his people— happens only as the Holy Spirit convinces and transforms. Settling for anything less does violence to the Bible.

It is probably true that many Christians who embrace fundamentalism aren't aware of its errors. They sincerely support beliefs they think essential to the Christian faith. An illustration will show what we mean. A bright young woman who was a member of our discussion group and who had always thought of herself as a fundamentalist was surprised to learn that some things she thought necessary for Christian discipleship are actually not required at all. Like some others in our group, she had regarded the Bible as a collection of divine information to accept without question.

Many in our group shared similar memories of how they had struggled to escape fundamentalism's rigid requirements. They recalled times when parroting fundamentalist beliefs about creation and other things about the Bible had stunted their learning and blocked robust discipleship.

In fact, in our group there was a measure of lingering resentment against how parts of the Bible had been taken out of context to prove fundamentalist teachings. Some remembered times when they were required to accept beliefs without regard for what those beliefs did to them as persons needing freedom to think about their faith. Instead of being taught to think critically and become mature in discerning the Bible's meaning, they felt constrained to embrace without question the assertions of fundamentalism. They were just supposed to shelve their own minds.

Our discussion group identified four specific reasons "why the chapter matters" for the church and Christian discipleship.

First, Christians in all ages have understood that the primary purpose of Scripture is to lead God's people in worship and obedience. So to turn the Bible into some kind of textbook filled with objective facts strips it of its divine mystery and power.

Second, the Bible has been the companion of Christians in their quest to be Jesus' faithful disciples. Its purpose is *not* to be a book of science or history. It is to be read and studied by believers to mold them in the image of Jesus Christ. Persons who are not Christians will not "get it"; the Holy Spirit has not opened their spiritual eyes. Did not Jesus tell us plainly that the world cannot receive the Holy Spirit "because it neither sees him nor knows him" (John 14:17)?

Third, the Bible is the Holy Spirit's book to the church. Through the Holy Spirit, the Bible faithfully communicates a faithful God to his not-so-faithful people. Turning the Bible into an objective, stand-alone document subverts the agency and primacy of the Spirit. Objectifying the Bible undercuts one of the Wesleyan-Holiness tradition's most cherished doctrines: the witness of the Spirit. The Holy Spirit is the cause behind Scripture and its authoritative interpreter in the church and personal lives of believers.

Fourth, placing the Bible's authority in the book itself, as fundamentalism does, has dangerous implications for the church, especially for discipleship. If the Bible consists of objective data generally accessible to human reason, then what need is there for the Christian community, for Scripture to be read and interpreted within the fellowship of the Holy Spirit? That is how the church has historically understood the interpretation of Scripture. Otherwise, anyone, left to his or her own devices, can just "figure out" the Bible alone. The body of Christ becomes unimportant. If, as the fundamentalist doctrine of Scripture implies, believers and unbelievers stand on equal footing when it comes to understanding the Bible, then the role of the Holy Spirit and the church pretty much disappears.

Some might say, "Well, viewing the Bible on the order of an objective scientific document is preferable to the subjectivity that plagues Bible reading today." But those are not the only options. The church of Jesus Christ, guided by the Holy Spirit, is the proper context for reading the Scriptures aright.

THE HARMONY OF SCIENCE AND THE CHRISTIAN FAITH

Fred Cawthorne, PhD

■ As we explore nature through science, our Christian faith and understanding can be enhanced by the elegance, vastness, and majesty of creation. Throughout my education, and as I continue to explore science through research and teaching, I am constantly amazed by the harmony that can be found between science and the Christian faith.[1] Additionally, the Wesleyan tradition[2] has provided a theological context in which to affirm historic Christian doctrine while engaging in legitimate science without compromise. As we explore aspects of the harmonious relationship between science and Christianity, my hope is that the God of All Truth will foster in his people a renewed sense of reverence, wonder, and awe. We may confidently join with Scripture in affirming "what was from the beginning, what we have heard, what we have seen with our eyes, what we have looked at and touched with our hands, concerning the Word of Life" (1 John 1:1, NASB).

Rooted in scientific advances, modern technology permeates much of our lives and provides a constant reinforcement of well-established scientific theories. One of the main reasons for the success of science is its overarching requirement that all theories must be validated or rejected on the basis of experiments. This approach works to keep the sciences from becoming a disconnected assortment of ideas and subjective opinions. It constantly requires that even the most cherished theories remain open to being proved wrong. Although the discoveries of science can be misinterpreted and misrepresented, if we affirm that creation is the work of God, then the findings themselves (the actual data) will be compatible with the Christian faith.

Here is how we will proceed. *First*, focusing on the transcendence and immanence of God, we will examine a possible common context in which science harmonizes with some essential Christian beliefs. *Second*, presenting some recent advances in cosmology and modern physics, a scientific description of time and space will be presented that resonates with the Christian doctrine that God the Creator is transcendent and that he created the universe out of nothing. It follows that in light of God's transcendence, our knowledge of God comes only through divine initiative, and our participation in God's life occurs *in* creation, a life revealed and made accessible through the incarnate Christ. *Third*, the fine-tuning of the laws of nature, without which life could not exist, further demonstrates God's gracious providence. On the most basic level, modern science has demonstrated that nature is not deterministic. God continuously upholds and sustains creation at every moment. *Fourth*, to conclude, we will consider scientific evidence supporting evolutionary theory and explore the consistency of these observations with the Christian faith.

The Transcendent God Revealed Through Creation

Christianity has long affirmed that God is both fully transcendent (wholly other) and fully immanent (revealed, active, and encountered in creation). The Nicene Creed begins, "We believe in God the Father Almighty, maker of heaven and earth." To reduce God to what is created is to deny his transcendence; it results in idolatry.

Unfortunately, it is possible to elevate nature (the created order) and science to a place of deity. But those of us who profess faith in Christ are subject to other forms of idolatry. One instance involves yielding to the temptation to separate God from creation by downplaying Jesus' full humanity, and hence the full revelation of God in Christ. The danger lies in elevating the spiritual as superior to the physical, just as the ancient gnostics did, but which the Bible refuses to do. A corollary temptation is refusing to let the physical creation freely tell its story by imposing on it arbitrary and faulty spiritual interpretations.

For those of us in the Wesleyan tradition, an affirmation of the full transcendence and immanence of God is essential. This entails an honest engagement with the creation encountered through the sciences. Although science in John Wesley's day was approached differently than it is today, he embraced an integrated view of science and Christianity. In fact, Wesley experimented with electricity and even compiled a book of natural philosophy (science) for his ministers.[3] Wesleyan scholar Randy Maddox notes that when there was a perceived conflict between *scripture* and *experience*, Wesley's approach was not to debate which was more authoritative but to engage "in the difficult (and often lengthy) reconsideration of his *interpretations* of *both* of these—and of tradition—often prodded by alternatives defended by others, until an interpretation emerged that *did justice to all*."[4] One consequence of this is that in the Wesleyan tradition, science is free to do its legitimate work, unimpeded by theological biases.

Although it is not the role of science to prove or disprove Christian doctrine, let us now explore some of the amazing discoveries made by modern science, seeking to catch a glimpse of the "one God and Father of all, who is above all and through all and in all" (Eph. 4:6).

Modern Cosmology and the Transcendence of God

In light of scientific discoveries that sometimes seem to challenge our beliefs, it is often the case that a better understanding of these discoveries can actually strengthen orthodox faith. For example, Christian tradition has long affirmed that God transcends space and time, that the universe was created *ex nihilo* (out of nothing)[5] and that the universe is fully dependent at every moment on God's continual creative and sustaining work. Christian theology renounces deism, which teaches that God created the world, instilled his laws in nature, and then left the world to operate on its own without any continuing divine activity or interference. God's continued involvement in the world—his immanence—must be affirmed. The book of Colossians speaks of "all things hold[ing] together" in Christ (1:17).

Science is now revealing amazing things about the universe through experimental investigations that for many years would have been inconceivable. Consider the modern concept that space and time are linked and that they were created (from nothing) at the beginning. A major transition in understanding the early universe (cosmology) began with the appearance of a new picture of gravity. Although Isaac Newton's "law" of gravity explained the mathematical form of gravitational attraction, how gravity works remained a mystery for over two hundred years. It wasn't until the early nineteen hundreds that Einstein postulated that gravity is actually the warping of space itself. By that time, Newton's law of gravitation had demonstrated remarkable success with only a few known exceptions (for example, it failed to accurately predict details of Mercury's orbit). Einstein's theory explains these and other phenomena for which Newton's theory fails.

Einstein's general idea is that space itself (even "empty" space) is a "thing" that can be stretched and warped by massive objects like stars and galaxies. Objects such as our earth follow the curve in space created by our sun in much the same way as a marble would "orbit" around the depression created by a person standing in the middle of a trampoline. This warping also causes light to appear to bend (although it is following the shortest path), just as the straight path of a long distance airplane flight appears curved when viewed on a map of the earth. Although there are now many known examples of this effect,[6] the first experimental confirmation that the geometry of space is warped by gravity was discovered during a solar eclipse when starlight was observed curving as it passed near the sun.

Einstein's theory of general relativity also includes time as a fourth dimension, linking the three dimensions of space with time to form a single fabric of space-time. Since space and time are linked, time itself is also warped by massive objects, and time runs slower in a gravitational field. This may sound like science fiction, but the effects of this warping of time are observable by everyday technology.[7]

There is significant evidence that the actual space-time fabric of the universe is expanding. In 1912, a few years after Einstein's formulation of relativity, Vesto Slipher made an interesting discovery. When looking at the spectrum (the pattern of light frequencies) produced by galaxies, Slipher discovered that the spectrum of the light from distant galaxies was shifted toward longer (redder) wavelengths. In 1929, Edwin Hubble and Milton Humason used a combination of their own data and data from Slipher and others to correlate the redshift of a galaxy with its distance from earth. It was already known that light from moving objects will be shifted toward the red when the object is moving away, and toward the blue when the object is moving toward the observer. What Hubble found is that all galaxies appear to be moving away from earth (i.e., all spectra were redshifted no matter where they were), and the apparent speed of recession is roughly proportional to the distance the galaxy is from earth.

Since everything appears to be receding from us, and the earth is not at the center of the universe, the universe itself (i.e., space) is expanding. Compare this to drawing a pattern of dots on a balloon and then inflating it. From the perspective of each dot, all of the other dots appear to be receding and there are no special center dots. Also, from the perspective of a particular dot, more distant dots appear to be receding more quickly than closer dots. This explains why we see galaxies receding from us in all directions and why distant galaxies appear to be moving away more rapidly than closer ones.[8]

One of the most significant additional pieces of the expanding universe puzzle was discovered by accident in 1964. When testing a highly sensitive antenna system, Penzias and Wilson noticed "noise" coming from all directions. Thinking there was a problem with their equipment, they carefully cleaned it and tested their experiment. But the signal—the cosmic microwave background (CMB)—remained.[9] Although we cannot go back and watch the beginning of the universe, the CMB gives scientists a way to experimentally investigate the universe as it was long before the formation of stars and planets. Since its initial discovery, there have been much more sensitive measurements of the CMB. One such measurement has been made by the WMAP satellite (Wilkinson Microwave Anisotropy Probe).[10] Over the past seven years, this satellite has provided significant evidence for the "hot big bang" model. Because the universe is expanding, the CMB is light from the very early universe that has been "stretched out" (highly redshifted into the microwave frequencies) and still permeates all of space.

So space itself is expanding, not just the "stuff" in space. The specific pattern of the CMB spectrum also indicates that the universe began in an extremely hot, dense state.[11] By extrapolation, we conclude that in the beginning there was no space, not even empty space; there were no places, and there was no matter. Because space and time are so closely linked, there were also no times before the beginning. It doesn't make any sense to talk about what came before creation. Even questions about the cause become tricky. The Creator of the universe, therefore, must exist outside of space and time.

So modern cosmology helps us understand that God, the Creator, whom we know by faith, transcends space and time. It also helps explain that space and time were created from "nothing" in the truest sense of the word. These conclusions are consistent with both Scripture and Christian tradition. For example, Augustine concluded that God is "the Maker of all time"[12] "'I am the Alpha and the Omega,' says the Lord God, 'who is and who was and who is to come, the Almighty'" (Rev. 1:8, NASB). God is, "I AM WHO I AM" (Exod. 3:14, NASB), a name Jesus attributes to himself: "Before Abraham was born, I am" (John 8:58, NASB). "All things came into being through Him, and apart from Him nothing came into being that has come into being" (1:3, NASB). This remarkable consistency between the Christian faith and modern cosmology does not "prove" that God was the ultimate cause of creation, but it does demonstrate that legitimate science is consistent with Christian doctrine.

Fine-Tuning of the Universe

As we have seen, the transcendence and immanence of God provide an interpretive framework for understanding the dependency of natural processes upon God's initiating and sustaining activity. The consistency between science and a Christian view of creation, however, does not end there. A closer look at the science of the early universe reveals many details that had to be "just right" for the universe to have any chance to support life. It is as though the universe has been intentionally fine-tuned.[13] This fine-tuning suggests the work of a Creator.[14] Without it, we would not have a universe that allows atoms or chemistry or planets, let alone complex biological life.

One example involves a resonance that allows stars to make carbon and other heavier elements necessary for all life. The concept of resonance is familiar because it forms the basis for all musical instruments. Think of a piano string. We know there are certain factors (like the string's mass and tension) that cause it to produce a certain note. The nucleus of the carbon atom has a resonance that is conceptually similar, and it happens to be just right for stars to make the chemical elements required for life. If this occurred accidentally, it would be like picking up a random piece of string, stretching and plucking it, and obtaining middle C. Without such precise tuning of the fundamental forces of nature, the universe would contain only hydrogen, helium, and some lithium, making life (intelligent or otherwise) completely impossible.

This does not prove God created the universe, but it is hard to ignore the appearance that the universe is designed to support life. One who denies the work of God in creation must go to great lengths to explain away the apparently intentional fine-tuning in creation.[15]

Upholding and Sustaining: The Rule of God over Nature

Could God have just caused a big bang (whatever that actually means outside of time), fine-tuned the universe, and then let it proceed without his intervening activity, eventually producing intelligent life as the result? Christian doctrine, as we have seen, answers no and affirms God's continuing creative and directing presence (Acts 17:28; Col. 1:17). How does science answer?

Around the same time that Einstein was working with relativity, light, and energy, another monumental paradigm shift was taking place in physics. Quantum mechanics was revealing the dual nature of light and matter. Instead of being treated as simply a tiny *particle* of matter, small objects such as electrons must also be treated as *waves* of potential. As a consequence of the wave nature of matter, we can't know where the electron is before it is measured. We can only know the probability of finding it at a certain location.

One of the best-tested theories in all of physics, quantum theory, answers fundamental questions such as why electrons in atoms don't rapidly spiral into the nucleus. For scientists, a disturbing philosophical consequence of quantum mechanics is that in a quantum experiment, we can know only the probability of a certain outcome. This is true even if the initial conditions are precisely known. It isn't that we don't yet know enough to predict the outcome with certainty. Instead, we know very well that we can never set up an experiment that will let us know with absolute certainty what will happen.

The consequence of all this is that the old picture of a deterministic universe, where the initial setup determines everything that follows, is simply not valid.[16] On these grounds, a creator such as the deists picture, who in advance determines the details of the universe and sets them in motion, would in fact be "rolling the dice." Given quantum uncertainty, a god no longer involved in the creation, who guides nothing, could not reasonably expect intelligent life to occur. Quantum mechanics makes it impossible to determine everything in detail from the beginning. On the other hand, if as historic Christian doctrine affirms, God had a plan for creation that included the appearance of intelligent life, then on the grounds of quantum mechanics we are led to confess that God has been active throughout the whole process, just as the Bible declares. This sheds light on Jesus' statement, "My Father is working until now, and I Myself am working" (John 5:17, NASB).

Not only did God create the universe out of nothing in the beginning, but he continually calls it out of nothing at every moment. All moments of creation are God's gracious gifts. Our knowledge of God comes only through the continuous divine initiative we call prevenient grace. Without God's upholding and sustaining presence, the universe would cease to exist. "In Him all things hold together" (Col. 1:17, NASB). Indeed, he "upholds all things by the word of His power" (Heb. 1:3, NASB).

Evolution

Given that God is continually working in and through creation, let us consider some of the facts that have been discovered through amazing advances in genetics and molecular biology. Over the past twenty years, the human genome (an organism's comprehensive hereditary information) has been mapped. Genetic factors contributing to diseases such as cystic fibrosis have been identified, and rapidly advancing DNA-sequencing technologies are increasingly being used to assist in drug development and discovery.

Throughout this process, substantial and comprehensive evidence supporting the evolutionary principle that life is related by common descent has been uncovered. Many Christian scientists claim that the theory of evolution is essential for the science of biology. At the same time, they regard the findings of evolution to be in harmony with their faith, rather than in conflict with it.[17] For example, Francis Collins, an experienced geneticist, former leader of the Human Genome Project, and current director of the National Institutes of Health, finds harmony between Christian truth and a scientific understanding of evolution. He writes, "Believers would be well advised to look carefully at the overwhelming weight of scientific data supporting the view of the relatedness of all living things, including ourselves."[18]

Many of the discoveries of evolution are consistent with what the Bible teaches (e.g., we are creatures: "For He Himself knows our frame; He is mindful that we are but dust" [Ps. 103:14, NASB]). While much work is still underway, there are a great (and growing) number of consistent examples from independent sources in the fossil record, genetics, biochemistry, geology, and biology that provide support for evolutionary theory. Although we should continue to evaluate the interpretations and conclusions drawn from the data,[19] as Christians seeking truth we should also be open to consider all the evidence. The specialness of our creation as humans comes from God alone and is ultimately revealed and expressed in the full humanity (and full deity) of our Lord Jesus Christ. Our faith is not attached to a specially created biological status within creation. Rather, our faith must be "rooted and fixed in God."[20]

In *The Language of God: A Scientist Presents Reasons for Belief*, Collins outlines a compelling argument for evolution and common descent.[21] For example, there is a gene in most mammals that is part of the process that allows them to produce their own vitamin C, but this gene (called a GLO sequence) is non-functional in humans. This is why sailors would get scurvy if they did not eat fruit during long voyages.

The deactivated gene (called a pseudogene) has suffered several mutations that prevent it from functioning, even though it has similar encoding and is in the same position as the functional gene in other mammals. It could be argued that humans could have produced vitamin C at one point, but a mutation has disabled the gene. The problem with this explanation is that all primates have this deactivated GLO sequence, strongly suggesting that the original mutation occurred in a distant ancestor of all primates (including humans). It is highly unlikely that the same deactivating mutations have occurred in all primates independently while the GLO sequence in other mammals remained intact.[22] But this does not mean that we are descended from current primates (e.g., monkeys). God's work in and through the hereditary processes of creation (granting the necessary freedom)[23] over vast amounts of time has "created an enormous gulf between us and any ancestors we share with other primates."[24]

Let us consider how this evidence is consistent with the Christian faith. *First,* evolution by no means contradicts the fact that God is the Maker of heaven and earth and that he has been actively guiding and sustaining the universe for all time. If we say that God cannot create through a gradual, progressive process such as evolution, then we limit God's transcendence and immanence. The authority of God over nature ("Who then is this, that even the wind and sea *obey* Him" [Mark 4:41, NASB, emphasis added]), his full participation in nature (Christ is fully human), and his gracious empowerment of nature[25] (of which we are part) are all consistent with a gradual, progressive creative process. *Second,* attempts to use the science of evolution to disprove God's existence are fundamentally flawed.[26] Discovering a "natural" process that reveals the gradual development of life does not contradict the fact that God creates, empowers, and upholds nature at every moment. On the contrary, such a discovery points to the consistency, continuity, and integrity of God's ongoing work over, in, and through creation. *Third,* we know that evolution cannot provide an ultimate explanation for life. The fine-tuned laws of nature do not originate from an evolutionary process although they are a prerequisite for biological evolution. Without chemical elements such as carbon, for example (as we have seen, carbon would not be present in the universe without fine-tuning), an evolutionary process is impossible. *Fourth*, we may faithfully affirm that creation was not finished in the beginning but was the start of a process through which God's creative and redemptive work continues toward a goal (*telos*), which is "new creation."[27] "For we know that the whole creation groans and suffers the pains of childbirth together until now" (Rom. 8:22, NASB).

Consideration of evolution should deepen our affirmation that God works above, in, and through creation; it should strengthen, not threaten, our faith. It should help us better understand God's transcendence and immanence. Jesus Christ is Lord of *all*!

Conclusion

As Christians we are called to worship God alone, not science, the Bible, reason, experience, or Christian tradition. But God can use all these instruments to make himself known as being above all (transcendent) and in all and through all (immanent) (Eph. 4:6). Although it is important to humbly recognize possible errors in our understanding, if we proceed carefully, all of these can work together holistically. Specifically, as we have seen, scientific findings can strengthen our trust in God instead of undermining it.

Instead of opposing free scientific pursuit, Christians should encourage scientific discoveries and learn from them. Science can help us understand more fully that "the earth is the LORD's, and all it contains, the world, and those who dwell in it" (Ps. 24:1, NASB). Theologian Jürgen Moltmann notes that "wisdom does not spring directly from experience. It is the fruit of the reflective handling of experiences."[28] By God's grace, a "reflective handling" of science can indeed produce wisdom. The depths of God are limitless, yet God continually draws us beyond where we have arrived in our journeys and into an ever expanding knowledge of him. We must not permit the point at which we have arrived—our current knowledge and understanding—to set the boundary for what God wants to teach us through numerous sources. Legitimate science is one of those sources. Let us not permit anything to force an unnecessary conflict between the Christian Scriptures and good science. Instead, let us pray that God will constantly renew and expand all dimensions of our knowledge and Christian discipleship. Let our lives echo the words of the apostle Paul: "Oh, the depth of the riches both of the wisdom and knowledge of God! How unsearchable are His judgments and unfathomable His ways!" (Rom. 11:33, NASB). Thanks be to God that he, "who said, 'Light shall shine out of darkness,' is the One who has shone in our hearts to give the Light of the knowledge of the glory of God in the face of Christ" (2 Cor. 4:6, NASB).

WHY IT MATTERS
(Chapter 6)

Rick Power, MA

Speaking as a parish minister, I want to use a personal account as the setting for my explanation of why Dr. Cawthorne's chapter "matters."

I was speaking to a group of teenagers during a weekend retreat. During a question-and-answer session, the students could ask questions about whatever was on their minds. We talked about drug and alcohol abuse, popular culture, sexual purity, sports, and a variety of other topics. Then a young lady raised her hand and asked, "What do you think about dinosaurs?"

Now *that* was an interesting way of asking the big question about the relationship between faith and science. How should I have answered that question?

If I had said I believed dinosaurs were created along with the rest of the animals about six thousand years ago, that they coinhabited the earth with human beings, that they were taken into the ark with Noah, then died off after the flood, I would have pleased some of the students in the audience—those who believe the Genesis accounts of creation require us to believe in a young earth.

If I had answered by saying that science has proven dinosaurs roamed the earth 65 to 220 million years ago, that human beings evolved much later, and that the Genesis accounts of creation were not intended to be taken as scientific descriptions, I might have pleased a different group of students—those who believe in theistic evolution.

Or I could have taken a mediating position that interprets the "days" of Gen. 1 as vast aeons of time, allowing for the creation and extinction of dinosaurs long before the sixth "day" of creation when God formed Adam from the dust of the ground. This answer would appeal to those who want to reconcile the scientific evidence for an old earth with the biblical account of a six-day creation.

But I didn't offer any of these responses. Instead, I answered, "You will be told by many people that your Christian faith is not compatible with belief in science. You should never accept this. If you're going to be thinking persons who seek truth wherever it can be found, you should embrace and value the discoveries of science even as you maintain your faith in Jesus Christ and your confidence in the Bible as the inspired Word of God. There are Christians who believe the first chapter of Genesis is a literal description of the way God created the earth and all living things. There are also Christians who believe the creation account is a poetic description of creation, not meant to be taken literally. Some of these folks believe the days of creation were long periods of time, not twenty-four-hour days. And some think God used evolutionary processes to create the advanced forms of animal life and human beings.

"The important thing to understand is that all these groups of people, in spite of their differing views, are born-again Christians. They love God and uphold the authority of Scripture. And one thing about which there is complete agreement is that God is the Creator and Sustainer of everything in the universe. You should never say that those who disagree with you are less than Christian or that they don't believe God's Word."

Of course, if Wesleyans were fundamentalists, I would have been constrained to answer the young lady's question differently. I would have told the students they are required to interpret Genesis literally and to reject as false any scientific evidence that appears to be in conflict with a literal reading of Scripture. Along with Dr. Cawthorne, I'm grateful that I don't have to respond that way to questions about faith and science.

As Wesleyans, we are unalterably committed to the full inspiration and authority of the Old and New Testaments. But we also believe that God enables us to apprehend truth by means of our Spirit-aided reason. While we do not exalt reason or experience above Scripture, we recognize that the Bible was written by persons who reflect the prescientific world-view of their historical contexts.

For example, the Bible's descriptions of sun, moon, and stars suggest a geocentric cosmology, with heavenly bodies moving across the canopy of the sky while the earth remains stationary on its foundations. The research of astronomers Copernicus and Galileo proved this view to be in error. Some church authorities condemned their scientific findings because they allegedly contradicted the testimony of Scripture. It was forbidden to publish any works that postulated the mobility of the earth or the immobility of the sun. But in time, the heliocentric solar system was established as scientific fact. We then adjusted our understanding of biblical passages that assumed a different cosmology.

Isn't it interesting that we're no longer troubled by this apparent contradiction between science and Scripture? Because we look to the Bible for theological truth about Jesus Christ and the kingdom of God, we don't require it to speak authoritatively on matters of science. Just as the church came to terms with the reality of a heliocentric solar system, we will also make our peace with evidence for evolution. Theistic evolution is a position that honors the biblical witness while also recognizing the overwhelming scientific evidence for evolutionary theory.

For the sake of church unity, I hope we can agree to disagree about difficult questions of science and faith. But because Wesleyans are not fundamentalists, we are open to readings of Scripture that allow us to embrace the discoveries of science while reverencing the profound truths of the Word.

I long for people to be both fully committed to Christ and intellectually honest. If we teach our young people that their only option is to treat the Bible as a textbook of science, we will cause many of them eventually to have an unnecessary crisis of faith. They may reject the Christian faith as untenable in light of the clear evidence of scientific discovery. But if we show people how the Bible is intended to be God's revelation of all things necessary to salvation, then as Dr. Cawthorne has shown, we'll promote freedom to appreciate all the ways science is unfolding the truth of God in the book of creation.

ON "BEING CHURCH"
A WESLEYAN UNDERSTANDING OF UNITY IN DIVERSITY

Mary Lou Shea, ThD

■ I . . . beg you to lead a life worthy of the calling to which you have been called, with all humility and gentleness, with patience, bearing with one another in love, making every effort to maintain the unity of the Spirit in the bond of peace. There is one body and one Spirit, just as you were called to the one hope of your calling, one Lord, one faith, one baptism, one God and Father of all, who is above all and through all and in all *(Eph. 4:1-6).*

With these verses John Wesley began his sermon "Of the Church." By choosing these verses to give his vision of Christ's community on earth, Wesley made clear his intention to hold his fellow believers to a high standard. Indeed, Paul's words call for a commitment that requires more than fallen and frail humanity can achieve on its own. As the body of Christ, we are called to live above the normal expectations—or even the wildest dreams—of Adam's unredeemed sons and daughters. We are called to live as those who have been redeemed by God's grace, and whose model is the Savior. Christians are urged to live lives worthy of Christ's sacrifice (Eph. 4:1; 2 Thess. 1:5, 11). We, the church, are to be humble, gentle, patient, hopeful, faithful, and forgiving. We are to bear with one another in love.

As Christ's beloved, we must see each other—and the whole world— through Christ's eyes (2 Cor. 5:14-16). We are to offer a respectful and tolerant welcome even to those we might find unlovely or argumentative or obstinate or fearful. And we are to offer that welcome with a genuine love that forgives and encourages and offers gracious correction when needed (1 Thess. 5:14; 1 Pet. 1:22). We are to live this way, daily, through times of concord and times of lively disagreement. At the core of who we are, there is "one body and one Spirit . . . one hope . . . one faith, one baptism, one God and Father of all" (Eph. 4:4-5).

This being true, it seems that as Christians we are supposed to live impossible lives. Were it not for God's enabling Spirit, the New Testament standard for life in the church would be impossible. Indeed, we in Christ's church often fall victim to the shameful belief that we are our own and that the church is ours to control. It is not. To be the church, its members must always remember that the church belongs to Christ. Selfish, private, and divisive standards must not be permitted to prevail. Instead, we must struggle against our own limited desires and perceptions and strive to embody the standards Christ has established for his people (Rom. 14:10-12). For example, we must reject the death-dealing power of fear or the urge to think of ourselves as the sole or chief authority on God's designs for his kingdom. Instead, members of Christ's body must demonstrate humility, gentleness, and forgiveness. They must forbear one another and be filled with shared Christian hope for the kingdom's consummation. Unless unity characterizes Christ's body, we who are its members can make no legitimate claim about loving God (1 John 4:20-21). Unless we love our sisters and brothers in Christ, we walk in darkness, sully Christ's name, and lose our witness to the world (2:9-11).

What Is Church?

The New Testament makes clear what being the church means, what it means to honor God and own his plan to redeem creation. The features of the

church largely describe what is expected of Christian character. But the New Testament also gives attention to early organizational patterns meant to preserve unity. We hear of presbyters (elders) and overseers (from the Greek *episcopoi,* also translated "bishops"), both of which meant the same thing (Acts 14:23; Phil. 1:1; Titus 1:5-7; 1 Pet. 5:1). Paul and Barnabas, for example, appointed presbyters or elders over the churches of Lystra, Antioch, and Iconium (Acts 14:23). Later, Paul instructed Titus to ordain presbyters in every town where a church had been established (Titus 1:5). Elders or presbyters were the pastors or ministers of the congregations, chiefly responsible for the pure ministry of the Word. There were also deacons, ministers of benevolence, whose responsibility was to minister to the needs of widows and orphans and to distribute food and goods among needy members of the church (Acts 6:1-6; Phil. 1:1; 1 Tim. 3:8). Paul describes the qualifications for each office in 1 Tim. 3:1-13 (cf. Titus 1:5-9). Common to requirements for both offices was a love for the church and a possession of stellar faith and integrity as shown in all relationships.

The early Christians were not known for their beautiful buildings or impressive programs. Their defining interest was to tell the story of Jesus and their own stories of redemption. Of course, the early church had its problems; it was comprised of persons who, under difficult circumstances, were learning to be Jesus' disciples.

While the church in the twenty-first century may properly long to embody the vitality of the New Testament church, this can't be done by simply re-creating its organizational structure and practices. In some parts of the world the church continues to be persecuted in ways similar to the early church. In other world areas the church faces no physical persecution and is no longer a small segment of the population (more than two billion people claim Christ as Lord). In all parts of the world the church must, in the power of the Holy Spirit, rise to the challenges of a twenty-first-century global society. Organizational needs differ from place to place. Such differences are minor when compared to our universal identity as members of Christ's body. John Wesley's appeal to Eph. 4:1-6 reminds us that we are children of "one God and Father." Whatever our incidental differences, the church, Wesley insisted, is composed of "all persons in the universe whom God has so called out of the world to entitle them" to achieve the measure of faith Paul describes in Ephesians. Wesley adds that Paul's description must apply to the church in all its dimensions, whether the universal church, a denomination, a local parish, or the Christian household.[1]

In line with Wesley's counsel, the Church of the Nazarene, as one example of a Wesleyan denomination, recognizes the church to be "the community that confesses Jesus Christ as Lord" and "the covenant people of God."[2] It is "the Body of Christ" called by the Holy Spirit to worship God and to live in unity and fellowship. This includes living in mutual accountability and serving the kingdom of God as one identifiable organization within the universal church.[3] Church membership includes "all spiritually regenerate persons, whose names are written in heaven."[4] Christians are providentially permitted to live in fellowship with and minister through voluntary associations such as the Church of the Nazarene.[5]

Neither the biblical mandate for the church, Wesleyan theology, nor the *Church of the Nazarene Manual* requires uniformity in all matters of thought and practice. As the New Testament makes clear, the church's unity resides in its confession of Jesus Christ as Lord of all and in a love that builds up the body of Christ. As Paul told the Roman and Corinthian Christians, there remain many subsidiary differences that must never be permitted to rise to positions of primary and divisive importance (Rom. 14:1-23; 1 Cor. 1:10-17). "The kingdom of God is . . . righteousness and peace and joy in the Holy Spirit. The one who thus serves Christ is acceptable to God and has human approval" (Rom. 14:17-18).

What Is Essential to the Faith That Unites?

From the beginning, the church universal has shared a small, but nonnegotiable, set of convictions: there is one God, who is almighty Creator and Sustainer, merciful, just and loving. There is one Lord, Jesus the Christ, Son of God. There is one Spirit, fully God and among us. There is one Lord, one faith, and one baptism. There will be a final judgment. We are to serve one another in love, live in harmony through the Holy Spirit, and share the gospel with all who have ears to listen. Aside from these central convictions, little else was required for membership in the church. Christians came from all parts of the known world; some were Jews and some were Gentiles. They spoke different languages and ate different foods. And they were admonished to allow for incidental differences while giving attention to what is essential to the faith (Acts 15:1-35; Rom. 14:20).

John Wesley, while constrained by the demands of a quickly industrializing England and organizational limits imposed by his role as a priest in the Church of England, was completely in line with the spirit of the early Christians. He relied upon Ephesians for his definition of the church as a faithful band of humble and loving believers who speak and live the gospel of Jesus Christ. Methodism was a church renewal movement, an attempt to reinvigorate the Church of England, which had too often become lost in political alliances and service to the socially privileged. Wesley wanted the Church of England to recover the true measure of Christian faith and practice. This would consist not of social rank, particular forms of worship or political power, but of transformed life and faithful service in Christ's name for God's glory.

Again, as one example of the Wesleyan family the Church of the Nazarene embraces a succinct and generously inclusive body of beliefs required for church membership. Failure to support these doctrines invites confusion and discontent. Its defining doctrines are believed to be "essential to the Christian experience."[6] Members believe (1) in the

Triune God; (2) that Scripture, inspired by God, contains all truth necessary to faith and Christian living; (3) that humanity is fallen and sinful; (4) that those who finally reject Christ and the salvation he offers will endure eternal separation from God; (5) that Christ came to redeem all persons and that those who accept him as Savior will rejoice eternally in his presence; (6) that believers can in this life live in such obedience to Christ that they are freed from the desire to sin (entire sanctification); (7) that the Holy Spirit is with believers and works with and through them; and (8) that final judgment will occur after Christ returns.[7] These doctrines are not novel in Christ's church; they continue to be instruments of transformation when embraced with conviction.

Language about the church that the apostle Paul, John Wesley, and many others use is distinctively countercultural. It is broad enough to leave space for manifestations of the free and wonderful works of God. Sin appears in many guises. Christian love appears in many forms. Each can be recognized if we will live close to Christ and in fellowship with the body of believers.

Living and speaking the gospel are often decided by a complex interplay of cultural, linguistic, and personal factors. Yet we recognize those lives spent in genuine service to God and humanity, even when we do not speak the language, understand the customs, or recognize the songs being sung. Love is easy to spot, welcome is easy to feel, and forgiveness is wondrous to experience.

What Is Unity?

We are enjoined by Scripture to make "every effort to maintain the unity of the Spirit in the bond of peace" (Eph. 4:3). This mandate rests upon faith in Jesus Christ as Lord and Savior and depends upon Christian character rather than any secondary beliefs Christians might have. The "unity of the Spirit" enables Christians to stand fast against slander, to suffer the loss of friends and family, and to endure poverty and the seizure of goods. "Unity in the Spirit" includes commitment to each other because of our prior commitment to the Lord. Jesus teaches us that those who are poor in spirit, those who mourn, the meek, the righteous, the merciful, the peacemaker, the persecuted, and the pure in heart will be called "great in the kingdom of heaven" (Matt. 5:3-19). All these entail a specific quality of relationship between persons. They reveal character and testify to virtue. We should not overlook the fact that Jesus' promise is not made to the smartest, to the best debater, or to the one who, based upon human wisdom, decides who should or should not be admitted to the body of Christ. God knows our understanding is imperfect at best and tragically flawed at worst. He warns us not to judge another's heart or status before him. The Lord has given us two commands: to love the Lord with all our heart, soul, mind, and strength, and our neighbor as ourselves—including those who might not fit our preferences for friend or neighbor. Everything rests upon our willingness to follow the Lord's commands (22:36-40).

John Wesley was deeply anguished over conflicts between the Church of England and the Methodists. He urged Christians to take to heart Jesus' rebuke of his disciples when they proudly announced they had forbidden someone to cast out demons because the man did not belong to their group. They did this even though the man was acting in Jesus' name. Jesus' response startled the disciples and alerted future generations of Christians: "Do not stop him; for no one who does a deed of power in my name will be able soon afterward to speak evil of me. Whoever is not against us is for us" (Mark 9:39-40). Jesus' admonition must be taken seriously. He has warned us not to hinder his servants just because they do not serve God in ways we approve. Instead, Jesus defends the outsider who faithfully performs deeds in his name. How much less, Wesley asked, should we who share a common faith disqualify each other over secondary matters? In Wesley's sermon "A Caution Against Bigotry," he warned against having "too strong an attachment to, or fondness for, our own party, opinion, church, and religion."[8] He urged his followers to recognize the faithful witness of others, even when they do not agree on all matters that *seem* essential to us. Perfectly faithful Christians might disagree about some aspects of morality, how God's grace works, and how best to worship.[9] Wesley pointed back to the New Testament church where unity was endangered because of disagreements over all manner of insignificant things. Observing Wesley's warning, contemporary Christians ought not to require uniformity of thought and action in matters not essential to the gospel. Unity in love is required.

Likewise, in its description of "Christian character,"[10] the Church of the Nazarene has offered guidance about how to live in unity. Members are enjoined to love God and neighbor, treat everyone with courtesy, and support other Christians. They should do what is good, support the church financially and by regular and devoted participation in worship services. Add to that avoiding all forms of sexual misconduct, avoiding "quarreling, returning evil for evil, gossiping, slandering, [and] spreading surmises injurious to the good names of others." Members are further counseled to be honest in all circumstances and to "abide in hearty fellowship" one with another.[11]

A Case Study of One Member of the Wesleyan Family: How Well Has the Church of the Nazarene Practiced Unity?

How well has the Church of the Nazarene practiced Christian unity? Imperfectly, as have all other Christian groups since the church's beginning, even though it has sought to embody unity in the Spirit. The denomination was formed by Christians from various denominations who thought their parent denominations had not been faithful to the New Testament call to Christian holiness, or who had failed the gospel by chasing the American dream of wealth and prestige at the expense of Christian simplicity. To make space for the diverse Christian traditions represented among the early Nazarenes, the denomination adopted an organizational structure that accommodated those backgrounds. The preamble to the government section in the denomination's *Manual* says, "The bases of unity in the Church of the Nazarene are those beliefs, polity, definitions, and procedures . . . articulated in the *Manual.* . . . The core of [its] unity is declared in the *Articles of Faith*."[12] This is set within the context of a representative form of governance that "avoids the extremes of episcopacy on the one hand and unlimited congregationalism on the other."[13] The church aims at allowing all voices to be heard and decisions to be made jointly.

Nazarenes have imperfectly embodied the Christian unity to which they aspire. They are often buffeted by social and political pressures that count against Christian unity. They welcome diversity but sometimes find it difficult to distinguish between what is essential for Christian faith and unity, and what is not. For example, they have sometimes allowed disagreements over the relationship between modern science and Christian faith and over the role of women in the church to become disruptive. They are not immune to the lure of the independent, "self-made" Christian or to the temptation to read the Bible as their private domain apart from the wisdom of the apostolic church.

How Should We Express Unity in the Twenty-first Century?

For Christians of all denominations, the answer to the question lies in our Christian heritage. *First,* we must in love embrace all persons who confess core Christian beliefs. *Second,* we must avoid imposing reading the Scriptures in ways that disrupt the body of Christ and that deny the diverse gifts God has given to our sisters and brothers. Paul said the church is not divided according to Greek and Jew, male and female (Gal. 3:28). We can expand his statement to include denominations and political parties. We should recognize that allegiance to any rule antithetical to the law of love is also antithetical to the kingdom of God. We ought to follow the biblical instructions that we conduct ourselves humbly and gently before each other. Gossip or slander or speaking evil of one another must not be given place among us. Divisions in the church, Wesley warned, rarely result in good being done or the gospel being advanced. "Cherished anger and resentment" and "alienation of affection" reveal a "want of love" in the church.[14] Where labels reign, the church suffers. Sisters and brothers become disenfranchised. Instead of this, let us be known by our love.[15]

WHY IT MATTERS
(Chapter 7)
Jeren Rowell, EdD

The chapter by Mary Lou Shea "matters" extensively in the body of Christ. The following is a practical "Amen!" to her counsel. It emerged from discussion between four laypersons—Julie Burch, Roger McCrummen, Cindy Thompson, and Dave Warner—and me.

Conflict is not only inevitable but also necessary for growth. As a pastor, anytime I heard married couples say, "Oh, we never fight," I thought one of two things must be the case. Either they are not being completely honest or they have grown so far apart there is nothing left to fight over. Conflict happens on the quest toward intimacy. As we grow closer to one another, we will discover that we have differences of opinion. Add to those differences strong feelings and there you have it—conflict! This is where growth in intimacy can happen as couples learn to navigate the conflicts in healthy ways through careful, loving, grace-filled communication. As the apostle encouraged the Colossian Christians, "Let your conversation be always full of grace, seasoned with salt, so that you may know how to answer everyone" (Col. 4:6, NIV).

What is true in marriage is also true in Christian congregations. The Scriptures regularly employ the image of marriage to teach about Christian community. This tells us that unity among Christians is no incidental imperative; it is essential for fulfilling God's mission in the world. Many people seem to think of "unity in diversity" as nothing more than tolerating our differences. However, when communities of faith become marked by authentic love, tolerance grows up to become a way of embracing diversity in response to grace and a strategy for nurturing the unity for which Jesus prayed. Our Lord prayed for the church,

"May they experience such perfect unity that the world will know that you sent me and that you love them as much as you love me" (John 17:23, NLT). Unity in the church is about much more than being *nice*; it is about modeling before a fractured world the living sign of *peace* that flows from *love*. When the church fails in unity, the wreckage becomes a barrier for the persons to whom we seek to bear Christian witness. Common are the testimonies today of people, especially young people, who walk away from the church partly because they do not see congregations acting much differently than the world. Against the advice of Paul to the Roman church, we have too often allowed ourselves to be "conform[ed] to the pattern of this world" (Rom. 12:2, NIV). Consequently, contemporary Christians often act very much like the consumers of our hedonistic age, exchanging the hard work of authentic relationships for the fast food of "church shopping."

The biblical call for unity among God's people is not a weak idea that passively asks, "Why can't we all just get along?" Unity in the church that becomes an authentic expression of the kingdom of God includes robust dialogue, perhaps even vigorous debate, but never contentious and polarizing speech making. When Christians disagree, as we often will, we are never given the careless luxury of minimizing or marginalizing the people with whom we disagree. Even when we disagree on matters considered essential, we are never free to harm another person by careless words. Occasionally I have heard someone say, "Well, I just tell it like it is. It's not my fault when people are offended." This attitude is unacceptable. In the body of Christ, love demands that we exercise grace-enabled discipline to say even hard things carefully, clearly, and humbly. The rule in our home is now a well-known axiom for our adult children: "In our family you can say anything, but you will say it with respect and care." This is quite different from the shrill rhetoric we often hear pouring from cable news and talk radio. Sadly, it seems that many of God's people are taking their cues from popular culture rather than from the

Scriptures for how people should be treated, especially those with whom we disagree. In conversation with a group of laypersons on this subject, someone noted, "We begin to fail when we stop seeing people as Christ sees them."

The commitment to unity in the midst of our differences matters because this is one of the more important ways the message of Christian holiness is (or is not) validated in the community of faith. When people from different backgrounds and life situations can come together, maintaining the "unity of the Spirit through the bond of peace" (Eph. 4:3, NIV), it becomes one of the more attractive ways the New Testament call to "perfect love" begins to live. Harmony is a wonderful way of talking about this. Musicians know that harmony doesn't happen when everyone sings the same note. It is achieved by integrating different notes that come together under good direction to create beautiful music. When unity in diversity characterizes the life of God's people in community, God is glorified and people are edified.

Many years ago I invited my congregation to think about Christian holiness in terms of love by citing a well-known passage in a little different way. Perhaps it offers us direction for discovering the joy of unity:

Holiness is patient, *holiness* is kind.

It does not envy, it does not boast, it is not proud.

Holiness does not dishonor others;

Holiness is not self-seeking, it is not easily angered.

Holiness keeps no record of wrongs.

Holiness does not delight in evil but rejoices with the truth.

Holiness always protects, always trusts, always hopes, always perseveres *(see 1 Cor. 13:4-7, NIV).*

May we live together as an answer to the prayer of our Lord—that our unity would become a winsome message of transforming love to a world far too acquainted with discord and strife.

A WESLEYAN UNDERSTANDING OF BIBLICAL AUTHORITY
THE FORMATION OF HOLY LIVES

Joel B. Green, PhD

■ Some years ago, I served as an associate pastor of a church that had replaced its aging King James Bible with a newer edition. This was one of those hefty volumes published in the mid-eighteen hundreds, and it had occupied a central place on the sanctuary altar since the founding of this local congregation. When this Bible was retired from regular use, it was placed in a museum-style display case located in the church foyer, where it was well protected. With the passing of time, although the display case received regular cleaning, the Bible on display was noticed less and less. My mind has returned to that image many times. I have found in it an object lesson for thinking about the doctrine of Scripture in many of our churches—a doctrine that shields the Bible from the ultraviolet rays and fingerprints of the modern age but does little to ensure that the Bible finds its way into the attitudes and habits of everyday Christian lives.

I wonder if there has ever been a time when it was easier to affirm that the Bible is God's Word while neglecting its divine claims on faith and life. Have we substituted our affirmations about the Bible for our engagement with its message? We have received the

Scriptures, not to place them in glass display cases for viewing, but to use them by reading, meditating, discussing, digesting, and practicing. Our views on the authority of Scripture are best proven in the character of our lives and not principally in the nature of our claims.[1]

The Authority of Scripture?

According to the Pew Research Center, some 63 percent of Americans believe Scripture is the Word of God. With a population of just over 300 million, that puts the number of people who share this belief in the neighborhood of 190 million. According to the Gallup Poll, these numbers have remained pretty consistent over the past couple decades. What is startling, then, is that only one-third of the American population reports they read Scripture at least once a week.[2] That's about 100 million people. Of course, there is a difference between reporting that one reads Scripture at least once a week and actually doing it. Moreover, we might admit, at least in principle, that it is possible for someone to live according to Scripture without actually reading it regularly. So we might say that these numbers do not tell us everything we want to know. Even so, we may find it astonishing that *claims* about the nature of Scripture apparently do not lead necessarily to even this most basic *practice* of opening the cover of the Bible and reading its pages.

The bottom line is that explicit affirmations about the Bible do not help us much to assess how or whether the Bible has an authoritative role in the life of the church. I am not suggesting that our doctrinal claims about Scripture are unimportant. Instead, I am suggesting that they are not enough.

Unfortunately, our situation has not been helped much by developments within the evangelical church. I refer to those evangelicals among whom the authority of Scripture has come to reside especially in the propositional content of the Bible and in affirmations concerning its trustworthiness. In the past century, American evangelicals have developed a well-nuanced vocabulary for speaking of Scripture—especially "infallibility" ("the full trustworthiness of a guide that is not deceived and does not deceive") and "inerrancy" ("the total trustworthiness of a source of information that contains no mistakes").[3] Such formulations as these have proven unhelpful for people committed to putting the authority of Scripture into practice in the life of the church. Although terms like "infallibility" and "inerrancy" do not represent well how we Wesleyans think about Scripture, my concern at this point lies elsewhere. I am urging that on the matter of *the use of Scripture in the life of the church*, such affirmations do not take us very far. This is because affirmations about the trustworthiness of the Bible (1) entail no guarantees regarding the faithful interpretation of Scripture and (2) extract no commitments from persons regarding their faithfulness to the Bible. In addition, these statements (3) misrepresent the nature of Scripture itself. In short, there is no necessary path from claims about the trustworthiness of the Bible to living lives oriented toward the Scriptures. Admittedly, this is a scandal, but it is nonetheless true.[4]

Let me take the first two claims together. If the authority of Scripture is best discerned in the lives (and not only the claims) of communities oriented around Scripture, then doctrines about Scripture are never enough. This seems clear, but let me illustrate it with ancient and contemporary examples. On the one hand, this truism is on display in the Gospels and Acts, where "the battle for the Bible" focuses not on *whether* Israel's Scriptures are to be taken seriously but on *how* they are to be understood within the framework of God's purpose and appropriated within the lives of God's people. Pharisees have one view of how to read God's aims in Scripture, the Jewish rulers in Jerusalem have another, and Jesus has still another. Yet all hold to the same authoritative Scriptures. Their struggle was not over how best to explain biblical authority. Rather, they could not agree on its faithful interpretation and embodiment. And this was a problem with such high stakes that differences of viewpoint surrounding the message of the Scriptures led eventually to the execution of one of its interpreters, Jesus. A more contemporary example is the Jehovah's Witnesses, who affirm biblical inerrancy and promote its literal interpretation. This viewpoint, however admirable, does not bring their theological commitments into line with the Christian faith as articulated either in the ancient creeds of the church or in the more specific doctrinal affirmations developed among Christians since.

What about my third claim, that affirmations of the trustworthiness or truth of the Bible fall short of the nature of Scripture itself? Remember, I am not denying the importance of doctrinal statements by which we give voice to the place of Scripture in God's revelation of himself, or the place of Scripture in the faith and life of the church. Instead, I am concerned about affirmations of inerrancy and infallibility that tend to reduce the witness of Scripture to its propositional content, and scriptural truth to what can be verified through observable data. This is the view that we can translate the ancient message of the Bible into its basic ideas, retranslate its message into contemporary words, and then supposedly show what the Bible teaches about God, human beings, and the whole of creation. The difficulties here are several. One involves the nature of the language and thought forms that make up the biblical materials. For example, Scripture embraces a complex and dynamic interaction of different sorts of language and modes of expression, including analogy, poetry, narrative, legislation, epistle, parable, and more. How are we to summarize the basic idea of a poem or a narrative or an account within a narrative? Certainly, we can add an explanation ("This poem is about . . ."). But this is hardly the same thing as grasping (and being grasped by) its meaning. And what definition of truth can be used to deduce whether a parable or oracle or poem is true? True with respect to what?

We should also recognize that statements about the truth of Scripture are likely to be accepted only by people who already believe that Scripture is true. That is, statements about the nature of the Bible as the Scripture of the church are not objective statements; they presume that belief is already in place. Theology, after all, is faith seeking understanding. Our judgments about the Bible arise from *within* the life and witness of the church; as a result, only those who are already predisposed to hear God's voice in Scripture are likely to do so. For others, the Bible might be interesting literature, a historical oddity, or a curious collection of stories and myths. People who read the Bible just as they would any other book are unlikely to embrace its view of God's reality merely because we Christians claim that the Bible gives us God's perspective on the world.

None of what I have said thus far should come as a surprise to people who count John Wesley as their spiritual and theological ancestor. Wesley preached that "true religion" does not reside in right doctrine alone. *Orthodoxy* ("right doctrine") cannot substitute for *orthopraxy* ("right action") and *orthokardia* ("right heart"). By naming these three, I know I am inviting us to walk a tightrope, since all three—right doctrine, right action, and right heart—must all be kept in balance.

After all, Wesley was committed to right doctrine, but there is more. For example, in his pamphlet "The Character of a Methodist," he sketches what does and does not distinguish those of his movement:

> The distinguishing marks of a Methodist are not his opinions of any sort. His assenting to this or that scheme of religion, his embracing any particular set of notions, his espousing the judgment of one man or of another, are all quite wide of the point. . . . We believe, indeed, that "all Scripture is given by the inspiration of God." . . . We believe the written word of God to be the only and sufficient rule both of Christian faith and practice. . . . We believe Christ to be the eternal, supreme God.[5]

In other words, when it comes to doctrine, people who follow in Wesley's footsteps affirm the faith of the Christian church as set forth in the creeds.

Wesley was also committed to right action, but there is more. He continues:

> Nor do we desire to be distinguished by actions, customs, or usages, of an indifferent nature. . . . It does not lie in the form of our apparel, in the posture of our body, or the covering of our heads; nor yet in abstaining from marriage, or from meats and drinks, which are all good if received with thanksgiving. Therefore, neither will any man . . . fix the mark of a Methodist here,—in any actions or customs purely indifferent, undetermined by the word of God.[6]

Right doctrine and right actions are important, but they are not what genuinely identify Wesleyan Christians. Hence, Wesley asks, "'What then is the mark? . . .' I answer: A Methodist is one who has 'the love of God shed abroad in his heart by the Holy Ghost . . . ;' one who 'loves the Lord his God with all his heart, and with all his soul, and with all his mind, and with all his strength.'"[7] Wesley makes just this point in his sermon "The Way to the Kingdom":

> A man may be orthodox in every point; he may not only espouse right opinions, but zealously defend them against all opposers; he may think justly concerning the incarnation of our Lord, concerning the ever-blessed Trinity, and every other doctrine contained in the oracles of God; he may assent to all the three Creeds,—that called the Apostles', the Nicene, and the Athanasian; and yet it is possible he may have no religion at all. . . . He may be almost as orthodox—as the devil . . . and may, all the while be as great a stranger as [the devil] to the religion of the heart.[8]

Wesley draws from Paul's words in Rom. 14 this emphasis on the inner life, the heart, where "righteousness, peace and joy in the Holy Spirit" (v. 17, NIV) take up lodging.

For us, then, the problem with a number of modern attempts to talk about the authority of Scripture is that they concentrate on what Wesley calls "right opinions." However sad or strange it might be, it

remains true that people are perfectly capable of making all sorts of far-reaching claims about the authority of the Bible while still holding the Bible at arm's length. The Bible needs to be removed from the glass display case for reading, meditating, discussing, and digesting. Our beliefs about the Bible are most on parade through right actions and right hearts.

The Scriptures of the Church

The authority of the Bible resides in its unique role of making accessible God's self-revelation to his people. To acknowledge the authority of Scripture is to admit that the Bible has its origin in God's desire to communicate with his people. It is to recognize that the essential function of the Bible for Christians is to reveal God to us. And it is to affirm that the aim of the Bible is realized when we have heard God address us through its pages.

We admit that the Bible can be read in many ways and by many different kinds of people. In fact, since the eighteenth century many have assumed that the Bible can be read productively by about anyone as long as he or she approaches it just as if it were any other book. However, to read biblical texts in this way is not the same thing as reading the Bible as authoritative Scripture. For more than two centuries, biblical scholarship has tended to work with biblical texts one at a time, primarily with reference to their production as human documents subject to the concerns of modern historical study. We have much to learn from this sort of investigation, but this is not the same thing as reading the Bible as authoritative Scripture. Some conservative evangelicals have turned to the Bible as a kind of doctrinal textbook from which to draw and organize statements about God and God's activity. This, too, is not the same thing as reading the Bible as authoritative Scripture.

How is this so? *First*, each of these approaches is quite capable of moving forward and being accepted without taking seriously the essential and overarching drama of Scripture. Working with the texts of the Bible in piecemeal fashion, reading a verse here or a verse there, even reading a whole book without reading the whole of Scripture, we fail to see that overall the Bible tells a single story that runs from Genesis to Revelation. This is the story of creation and fall, slavery and exodus, exile and restoration, and the coming of Christ to inaugurate God's new creation. This is the story of God, the God who created, liberated, and led—the same God who raised Jesus from the dead and poured out the Spirit on his people. If we do not grasp this overarching drama of Scripture, then we fail to see the larger mural of divine activity, we fail to see how the church fits into God's agenda, and we fail to understand who we are and the vocation of service to which God has called us.

Second, Christians do not come to Scripture as they would come to any other book. They do not come to Scripture to assess its historical basis or origin. Nor do they come to Scripture to summarize and organize its statements about God. True, Christians may do all of these things, but none of these represents a particularly Christian approach to Scripture. Put sharply, Christians come to Scripture to hear God's voice—that is, to hear and do God's Word. Affirming the authority of Scripture, then, can never be reduced to an intellectual exercise by which we count the Bible as trustworthy. In fact, claims concerning the Bible's trustworthiness that grow out of modern concerns for truth and verification rather than out of Scripture's own concerns and purpose are simply new ways for us to stand over the Bible. Attempts to protect the Bible assume that the aims of Scripture depend on human agency rather than on God's. Instead, what we need are gestures of openness, humility, submission, and obedience. Christian readers of the Bible want to become familiar with ancient peoples and their cultures. We honor being schooled in the biblical languages. We want to cultivate good skills for reading the Bible. What we who affirm Scripture's authority need even more, though, are such dispositions and postures as acceptance, devotion, attention, and trust.

To affirm the authority of Scripture is to adopt habits of reading and prayer that lead to the conformity of our thoughts, feelings, beliefs, and behaviors to God's will revealed in Scripture. We find here, in the pages of Scripture, who we are and what we are to become. Accordingly, we acknowledge and invite the ongoing work of Scripture's divine author as the One who desires to shape us as a community, the church, God's people.

For a particularly Wesleyan understanding of this way of thinking about Scripture's authority, we can turn to an often-cited comment Wesley made about the Bible in the preface to his "Sermons on Several Occasions":

> I want to know one thing,—the way to heaven; how to land safe on that happy shore. God himself has condescended to teach the way: For this very end he came from heaven. He hath written it down in a book. O give me that book! At any price, give me the Book of God! I have it: Here is knowledge enough for me. Let me be *homo unius libri* [a man of one book]. Here then I am, far from the busy ways of men. I sit down alone: Only God is here. In his presence I open, I read his book; for this end, to find the way to heaven.[9]

Notice the repetition, in the first and last sentences, of the phrase "the way to heaven." The aim of Scripture is to guide us in "the way to heaven." This "way" is not focused narrowly on eternal life, of course. For Wesley, it refers more broadly to the journey of salvation—from original sin to justification and new birth, and on to holiness. To embrace the authority of the Bible as people in our theological tradition means taking seriously both this aim of Scripture (to reveal the way to heaven) and these consequences of our reading Scripture (to find the way to heaven). Reading Scripture is tied to the journey of salvation. The Bible teaches "the way to heaven." And Wesley reads the Bible with this aim in mind—"to find the way to heaven." How may we know if the Bible is true? If it shows us the way to heaven. How do we know if we have stood under Scripture's authority? If our reading furthers our progress on the way to heaven.

Scripture's Authority

How does the Bible assert its own authority? It does so only rarely, and this presses us to distinguish between two kinds of authority: extrinsic and intrinsic. We accept statements carrying extrinsic authority not because the statement itself is compelling but because we grant the speaker the authority to make it. But if the statement itself is compelling, regardless of who made it, we recognize its intrinsic authority. Most Christians relate to the Bible by granting it some combination of intrinsic and extrinsic authority. Scripture itself presents its own *intrinsic* appeal in several ways—for example, calling upon our imaginations, reminding us of our commitments, asking us to consider reasoned arguments, urging us to engage in self-reflection on our experience as God's people. It persuades and convinces but rarely demands.

On the one hand, we find that as we give ourselves to life in the Spirit and to an engagement with Scripture, God works in our lives and imaginations. He leads us further into Scripture and we find the Bible more and more to be true. This means that what is needed most are people deeply embedded in faithful communities of discipleship, people in whom the Spirit is actualizing the Word of God and, thus, for whom the Word of God is authenticated. On the other hand, God speaks, and this is the basis for Scripture's authority. Through Scripture, God convinces us that things between himself and humanity—indeed, between God and all creation—are just as we find in Scripture. Embracing Scripture's authority, we are drawn into the story of Scripture and especially more deeply into relationship with Scripture's primary character, God himself.

In short, the authority of Scripture is less a demand and more an invitation to come and make our home in this story of God's ongoing and gracious purpose for his people. The authority of Scripture is an invitation to resist attempts at revising its words in order to make them match our reality. Instead, we make sense of our reality, our lives, within its pages and according to its story. To embrace Scripture's authority, then, is to allow ourselves to be shaped by it thoroughly and ultimately.

Precisely because Scripture is first and foremost about God, it draws its chief nature from God. If divine-human relations are based in God's generous initiative and sustaining faithfulness, culminating in the powerful, restorative activity of God on behalf of humanity, then how could the claims of Scripture ever be mistaken for a kind of divine trump card that God (or one of his spokespersons) plays when backed into a corner? If Scripture draws its character from God, how could the authority of Scripture be anything but a gracious gift, an expression of divine care?

Conclusion

It is never enough simply to think correctly about the nature of Scripture. Instead, embracing Scripture's authority is more about our character, our attitudes, as we come to Scripture. We recognize Scripture's authority when we approach it ready to be formed truly in relation to the God whose self-communication we hear in Scripture's drama. Scripture's authority is thus most visible among those whose lives embody God's address heard in and through Scripture.

WHY IT MATTERS
(Chapter 8)

Carla Sunberg, MA

We live in a time when an abundance of Christian media calls for our attention. Much of it affirms the Christian Scriptures, and in many ways Christian discipleship is fostered. Sometimes the Bible is used to give authoritative explanations of how God created the world. Often the persons making the arguments present their positions as though they are required by the Bible. The speakers do not pause to tell us their claims are closely tied to underlying doctrinal presuppositions and worldviews they have imposed on the Bible. As a result, many who hear the claims think they are receiving unvarnished interpretations of the Scriptures.

Sometimes laypersons have told me they simply want to "hear the Bible" without any theology or doctrine attached to it. They want to receive the Bible without it being associated with what others have taught in the past. "Just give me the simple truth," they say. Well, the "simple truth" is that when anyone interprets Scripture his or her interpretation is to some extent accompanied by doctrine. That cannot be avoided. No one approaches the Bible independent of some doctrinal or cultural perspective. Believing otherwise leads to confusion.

The objective "trustworthiness or truth of the Bible," as Joel Green labels it, is very popular. It is the notion that the Bible's truth or proof or trustworthiness is lodged in the Bible itself and that discovering its objective truth is what biblical authority is all about. Once achieved, you don't need to go any further. There is a widely held perception that this is *the* correct perspective on biblical authority. Many laypersons and pastors in Wesleyan denominations mistakenly think this understanding is consistent with Wesleyan theology. Joel Green has

shown us how far removed this popular understanding of biblical authority is from Wesleyan theology. In fact, for Wesleyans, the affirmation
of biblical authority rests primarily in whether or not its message suc-
ceeds, through the Holy Spirit, in transforming our lives and impacting
our world through holy living. This is finally where the "proof" of biblical
authority rises or falls—in the power of the gospel of Jesus Christ.

Too often, debates about "what the Bible says" become destructive in
the body of Christ, and the Bible's real purpose miscarries.

I want to offer a personal illustration of why Joel Green's chapter
"matters." As parents, my husband and I have tried to raise our daughters
to avoid seeing the Bible as something about which we should argue. Instead, we have tried to teach them that the goal of the Bible is to cultivate
a love for God and neighbor. Admittedly, in a complex world, putting this
goal into practice can be difficult. But both of our daughters now have a
passion for serving God and for helping others.

Our daughters attended a Christian school not informed by Wesleyan theology. Once during that school's spiritual formation week a special
speaker was invited to help the students grow in their faith. The whole
week was dedicated to preaching a particular perspective on the Genesis
creation story. Students were told that if they failed to accept the view of
creation being presented they would go to hell. Our daughters were being
subjected to an interpretation of the Bible that the Bible itself does not require. They were being submitted to a belief that the primary value of the
Bible resides in what it objectively teaches and to an interpretation loaded
with prior assumptions that even the speaker probably did not recognize.
Our daughters were witnessing the error against which Joel Green warns.

The warning against going to hell did not land its mark on our daughters because they were already being taught at home that
the Bible makes no such demands. They were able to
see that spiritual formation was not really what the
speaker was pursuing.

At the end of that year our oldest daughter wanted to run for school chaplain. She was told that she could not. The reason? She was a girl and the Bible, she was told, opposed women holding such positions. As a compromise, she was allowed to do all the work of the school chaplain. But a boy had to have the official title. The school officials who were imposing this interpretation of the Bible believed they were treating the Bible objectively. They were unaware of the doctrinal and cultural biases they were imposing on the Bible. Because our daughter was more concerned about the kingdom of God than she was with the title, she did the work.

Experiences like these illustrate that our understanding of biblical authority provides a blueprint for how we practice our faith, personally and in the body of Christ. In the Wesleyan tradition, what drives our understanding and our blueprint is Jesus' prayer, "Your kingdom come. Your will be done" (Matt. 6:10). Our primary interest in the Scriptures derives from our commitment to the kingdom here on earth, not to how the world came into existence or any other claim about the natural world or world history. We believe in the transforming power of the gospel of Jesus Christ, in the Spirit's empowerment for holy living. This broken world can be transformed. There, for us, is where the authority of Scripture is manifest.

As Wesleyans, it is important that we be able to articulate our perspective and recognize why we think and speak as we do. Rather than permitting our perspective to be co-opted by fundamentalism, we need to embrace our distinctive beliefs as Joel Green has stated them and ask the Holy Spirit to proclaim through us the message of Christian hope in a broken world. Let us renew our commitment to the Bible as living and active and breathing in our daily lives.

CONCLUSION

The contributors to this volume have shown that fundamentalism and Wesleyan theology share many commitments to orthodox Christian doctrine. They also share a love for righteousness. But the contributors have also shown that Wesleyan theology and fundamentalism hold significantly different convictions about some things, including how the authority of Scripture should be understood, how and where the Bible's meaning is most properly manifest, what must be believed to be "Christian," and how the Christian faith should relate to the natural sciences. The two approaches to the Christian faith are irreconcilable in these respects because of different loyalties and goals.

Much of what fundamentalism wants to defend as essential, Wesleyan theology considers nonessential. For example, for fundamentalists the integrity of the Old Testament would be undercut if Moses did not write the Pentateuch (the first five books of the Bible). Or for the authority of the book of Isaiah to be safeguarded, all of it must have been written by the eighth-century BC Isaiah of Jerusalem. By contrast, Wesleyans believe the meaning and importance of the Pentateuch and Isaiah have much more to do with understanding Israel's historic and often complex sojourn with the covenant-making God than with authorship. For that reason, Wesleyans want to learn all they can about how the Old Testament—and the New Testament—was formed. To take one more example, while fundamentalists insist that the creation stories in Genesis and modern science must be reconciled, Wesleyans read those texts in a manner that places no such demands upon the sciences, the Scriptures, or Christian life and thought.

As contributors have emphasized, Wesleyans have an unambiguous confidence that the Holy

Spirit will faithfully teach God's people how the Bible is unerringly sufficient for leading them in the ways of righteousness. The Spirit will speak through the Scriptures to teach the church how to be the body of Christ. He will use the Old and New Testaments to nurture Christian disciples, ever transforming us into the image of Christ and teaching us how to be faithful in Christian witness and mission. For Wesleyans the Bible's authority is inseparable from redemption and witness, and communion in the body of Christ. Valuing the Scriptures for any other reason is for Wesleyans of secondary importance.

These values are being affirmed and confirmed by college and university students who find the relational, communal, and lived-out quality of Wesleyan theology compelling. They are attracted by an understanding of the Scriptures and the Christian faith that places Christians in the world as emissaries of God's inaugurated kingdom. Fundamentalism's characteristic preoccupations don't well serve that passion.

Wesleyan theology is favorably positioned for the opportunities and challenges of the twenty-first century. A host of Wesleyan scholars— such as Elsa Tamez, Theodore Runyon, Diane Leclerc, and William Abraham—are demonstrating that Wesleyan theology contains an internal dynamic and freedom that makes it possible to remain true to historic Christian doctrine while creatively addressing the gospel to diverse cultures and worldviews. This dynamic helps us avoid paralyzing doubt on the one hand and religious and intellectual obscurity on the other.

Wesleyan theology can serve Christian evangelism in ways not accessible to fundamentalism. Its doctrine of the Scriptures and fidelity to historic Christian doctrine lets us address the gospel to persons who are informed about human, cosmic, and geological history, the natural and social sciences, and the world's religions and cultures in ways closed to fundamentalism.

We in the Wesleyan tradition have a responsibility and the resources needed for embracing the best that biblical scholarship has to offer and for processing the results of legitimate science. Let the young people in our tradition know that it offers them solid spiritual and intellectual warrant for becoming leaders in the sciences, in theological studies, in Christian ministry, in social and political service, in commerce, and in all venues graced by the risen, reigning, and coming Lord. And let them hear from all of us that the gospel of Jesus Christ and the veracity of the Scriptures can be incarnated there.

Faithful and creative stewardship of our heritage is called for. We owe such stewardship to our children who are as capable of learning and living the faith well as they are of learning and living it poorly. We owe it to students in our colleges and universities to whom we have promised that the Christian faith retreats to no intellectual ghetto. We owe it to a plurality of cultures and religions to which the gospel must be intelligibly proclaimed and winsomely incarnated. And we owe it to laypersons who wish to be well informed, to the Scriptures, to a broken world in need of the Savior, and most of all to our Lord.

NOTES

Introduction

1. John Wesley, "Catholic Spirit," in *The Works of John Wesley*, ed. Thomas Jackson (1872; reprint, Kansas City: Beacon Hill Press of Kansas City, 1986), 5:500.

2. Ibid., 492-504.

3. Martin E. Marty and R. Scott Appleby identify numerous types of fundamentalism currently observable in various religions. In this book we are dealing mostly with what Marty and Appleby identify as "North American Protestant Fundamentalism." Martin E. Marty and R. Scott Appleby, eds., *Fundamentalisms Observed*, The Fundamentalism Project, vol. 1 (Chicago: University of Chicago Press, 1994).

4. Wesley, "A Letter to a Roman Catholic," in *Works of John Wesley*, 10:86.

5. Anselm of Canterbury, *Proslogion*.

Chapter 1

1. James Barr, *Fundamentalism* (Philadelphia: Westminster Press, 1978), 1.

2. Nancy T. Ammerman, "North American Protestant Fundamentalism," in *Fundamentalisms Observed*, 4-8.

3. George M. Marsden, *Understanding Fundamentalism and Evangelicalism* (Grand Rapids: William B. Eerdmans Publishing Co., 1991), 1.

4. George M. Marsden, *Fundamentalism and American Culture: The Shaping of Twentieth-Century Evangelicalism 1870–1925* (New York: Oxford University Press, 1982), 3. Fundamentalism, Timothy Weber says, was organized "to defend orthodox Protestant Christianity against the challenges of theological liberalism, higher criticism of the Bible, evolution and other modernisms judged to be harmful to traditional faith," in *Dictionary of Christianity in America*, Daniel G. Reid, Robert Linder, Bruce L. Shelley, and Harry S. Stout, eds. (Downers Grove, Ill.: InterVarsity, 1990), 461.

5. Ernest Sandeen, *The Roots of Fundamentalism: British and American Millenarianism 1800-1930* (Chicago: University of Chicago Press, 1970), 132-61; Timothy P. Weber, *Living in the Shadow of the Second Coming: American Premillennialism 1875–1920*, enlarged ed. (Grand Rapids: Zondervan, 1983); Paul Boyer, *When Time Shall Be No More: Prophecy Belief in Modern American Culture* (Cambridge, Mass.: Harvard University Press, 1992), 80-112.

6. Sandeen, *Roots of Fundamentalism*, 103-31; Marsden, *Fundamentalism and American Culture*, 109-18.

7. David N. Livingstone, *Darwin's Forgotten Defenders: The Encounter Between Evangelical Theology and Evolutionary Thought* (Grand Rapids: William B. Eerdmans Publishing Co., 1987). See also Theodore Dwight Bozeman, *Protestants in an Age of Science:*

The Baconian Ideal and Antebellum American Religious Thought (Chapel Hill, N.C.: University of North Carolina Press, 1977).

8. See E. Brooks Holifield, *Theology in America: Christian Thought from the Age of the Puritans to the Civil War* (New Haven, Conn.: Yale University Press, 2003), 377-89.

9. Sandeen, *Roots of Fundamentalism*, 120-30. See also Bradley J. Longfield, *The Presbyterian Controversy: Fundamentalists, Modernists, and Moderates* (New York: Oxford University Press, 1991); D. G. Hart, *Defending the Faith: J. Gresham Machen and the Crisis of Conservative Protestantism in Modern America* (Phillipsburg, N.J.: P and R Publishing, 1994), 96-98.

10. Cited in William Gatewood Jr., *Controversy in the Twenties: Fundamentalism, Modernism, and Evolution* (Nashville: Vanderbilt University Press, 1969), 65.

11. See especially William R. Hutchison, *The Modernist Impulse in American Protestantism* (Cambridge, Mass.: Harvard University Press, 1976).

12. B. F. Haynes, "The Grudge of Philosophy Against Revelation," *Herald of Holiness,* 30 June 1920, 1. See Sandeen, *Roots of Fundamentalism*; Marsden, *Fundamentalism and American Culture*, 212-21; and Hart, *Defending the Faith*. See also George Dollar, *A History of Fundamentalism in America* (Greenville, S.C.: Bob Jones University Press, 1973), though this work is biased toward the fundamentalist position and indicates that group's antipathy toward the Wesleyan stance. Especially helpful is Paul Bassett, "The Fundamentalist Leavening of the Holiness Movement, 1914-1940: The Church of the Nazarene: A Case Study," *Wesleyan Theological Journal* 13 (Spring 1978): 65-91.

13. Morton White, *Social Thought in America: The Revolt Against Formalism* (New York: Viking Press, 1947). On broader issues see Christopher P. Toumey, *God's Own Scientists: Creationists in a Secular World* (New Brunswick, N.J.: Rutgers University Press, 1994); James Gilbert, *Redeeming Culture: American Religion in an Age of Science* (Chicago: University of Chicago Press, 1997).

14. Edward J. Larson, *Summer for the Gods: The Scopes Trial and America's Continuing Debate over Science and Religion* (New York: Basic, 1997); Michael Kazin, *A Godly Hero: The Life of William Jennings Bryan* (New York: Alfred A. Knopf, 2006).

15. Joel A. Carpenter, "A Shelter in the Time of Storm: Fundamentalist Institutions and the Rise of Evangelical Protestantism, 1929-1942," *Church History* 49 (March 1980): 62-75. William V. Trollinger Jr., *God's Empire: William Bell Riley and Midwestern Fundamentalism* (Madison, Wis.: University of Wisconsin Press, 1990); Joel Carpenter, *Revive Us Again: The Reawakening of American Fundamentalism* (New York: Oxford University Press, 1997); and Margaret Lamberts Bendroth, *Fundamentalists in the City: Conflict and Division in Boston's Churches, 1885–1950* (New York: Oxford University Press, 2005) illustrate the urban orientations of fundamentalism in the mid-twentieth century.

16. Hart, *Defending the Faith*.

17. Paul Carter, *The Decline and Rise of the Social Gospel: Social and Political Liberalism in American Protestant Churches 1920-1940* (Ithaca, N.Y.: Cornell University Press, 1956), 49, 55; C. Allyn Russell, *Voices of American Fundamentalism: Seven Biographical*

Studies (Philadelphia: Westminster, 1976), particularly the chapters on J. Frank Norris, John Roach Straton, and William Bell Riley, and for the latter see also Trollinger, *God's Empire*, 69.

18. See Nancy T. Ammerman's account of the division between "fundamentalists" and "evangelicals." "North American Protestant Fundamentalism," 4.

19. For an excellent history of the King James Bible see Alister McGrath, *In the Beginning: The Story of the King James Bible and How It Changed a Nation, a Language, and a Culture* (Harpswell, Maine: Anchor, 2002).

20. George Marsden, *Reforming Fundamentalism: Fuller Seminary and the New Evangelicalism* (Grand Rapids: William B. Eerdmans, 1987); Mark Ellingsen, *The Evangelical Movement: Growth, Impact, Controversy, Dialog* (Minneapolis: Augsburg, 1988), 93-106; Garth Rosell, *The Surprising Work of God: Harold John Ockenga, Billy Graham, and the Rebirth of Evangelicalism* (Grand Rapids: Baker, 2008). On issues regarding the KJV and other translations see Peter J. Thuesen, *In Discordance with the Scriptures: American Protestant Battles over Translating the Bible* (New York: Oxford University Press, 1999).

21. For an extended explanation of why Wesleyans cannot accept the fundamentalist doctrine of inerrancy, see W. Stephen Gunter, "Beyond the Bible Wars: Why Inerrancy Is Not the Issue for Evangelical Wesleyans," *Wesleyan Theological Journal* 46, no. 2 (Fall 2011), 56-69.

22. H. Orton Wiley, *Christian Theology* (Kansas City: Nazarene Publishing House, 1940), 1:173-75.

23. For Hooker, the authority of Scripture is that it contains all things necessary to salvation.

24. See Ralph Earle, "Wesley and the Methodists," *The Preacher's Magazine* (July 1959), 20-23.

25. W. T. Purkiser, "Keynote Address," 1958 Theology Workshop, 10 (Nazarene Archives, file 729-31).

26. See, for example, Ralph Earle, "Verbal Differences in Parallel Passages in the Synoptics and Their Implications for a Doctrine of Divine Inspiration," *Asbury Seminarian* (Spring-Summer 1954); Earle, "Wesley and the Methodists"; W. T. Purkiser, in *Exploring Our Christian Faith* (Kansas City: Beacon Hill Press, 1960), 60-80. See also John Cotner, "Report of the Study Group on the Holy Scriptures" (Nazarene Archives, file 729-31); Frank Carver, "The Bearing of Hermeneutical Issues on the Question of Biblical Authority," December 1-3, 1975 (Nazarene Archives, file 729-37).

27. Wiley, *Christian Theology*, 1:454-56. For an extensive treatment of the Wesleyan basis for understanding the relationship between the Christian faith and the natural sciences, see Randy L. Maddox, "John Wesley's Precedent for Theological Engagement with the Natural Sciences," *Wesleyan Theological Journal* 44, no. 1 (Spring 2009) 23-54.

28. Wilbur Mullen, in *Exploring Our Christian Faith*, 132. See similarly W. T. Purkiser, C. E. Demaray, Donald Metz, and Maude Stuneck, *Exploring the Old Testament* (Kansas City: Bea-

con Hill Press, 1955), 70-72; W. T. Purkiser, Richard S. Taylor, and Willard H. Taylor, *God, Man and Salvation* (Kansas City: Beacon Hill Press of Kansas City, 1977), 52-59. Also see Ronald Kirkemo, *For Zion's Sake: A History of Pasadena/Point Loma College* (San Diego: Point Loma Press, 1992), 297-98, 332-33; Ronald Numbers, *The Creationists* (New York: Alfred A. Knopf, 1992), 305-7.

Chapter 2

1. "Literary styles" here does not denote various genres of texts (poetry, proverbs, prose, history, etc.), but the individual ways of writing manifested by various authors within the same literary genre. For example, Paul does not write in the same manner as John.

2. The original manuscript penned by the writer. It is in later copies of the autographs, and copies of the copies, where variant readings emerge.

3. For instance, the Chicago Statement on Biblical Inerrancy states, "We affirm that inspiration, strictly speaking, applies only to the autographic text of Scripture."

4. The Textus Receptus is the Greek manuscript developed in the sixteenth century, beginning in 1522 with Ximenes' edition of the Hebrew, Latin, and Greek Bible, the Complutensian Polyglot. The work of Erasmus (1516), Stephanus (1546-51), and Beza concluded with the Elzevir brothers, whose 1633 edition contained the phrase "Textum . . . receptum," subsequently known as the Textus Receptus. This text consisted largely of later and less reliable manuscripts than are now available.

5. See McGrath, *In the Beginning*.

6. Detroit Baptist Theological Seminary, *Inspiration and Preservation of Scripture* (Detroit: Detroit Baptist Theological Seminary, 1996).

7. Thomas Merton, *Opening the Bible* (Collegeville, Minn.: Liturgical Press, 1970), 20.

8. Wesley, "Preface to the Explanatory Notes upon the Old Testament," in *Works of John Wesley*, 14:252. One should, by no means, conclude from what follows here that Wesley was anti-intellectual. One need only read his extended scholarly discussion with Conyers Middleton to see that Wesley was skilled in biblical scholarship: Wesley, "A Letter to the Reverend Dr. Conyers Middleton," in *Works of John Wesley*, 10:1-79.

9. Scripture references added throughout the citation.

10. Wesley's "tempers" would best be understood today as "temperament" or "character," an inner state of being.

11. "Conversation" means lifestyle, the manner in which one conducts one's life in the world.

12. Wesley, "Preface to the Explanatory Notes upon the Old Testament," in *Works of John Wesley*, 14:253.

13. Wesley, "A Roman Catechism," in *Works of John Wesley*, 10:90.

14. Wesley, "The Law Established Through Faith," in *Works of John Wesley*, 5:459.

15. "Man's human and worldly wisdom or science is not needful to the understanding of Scripture but the revelation of the Holy Ghost who inspireth the true meaning unto them that

with humility and diligence search [for it]." "Homily of Reading the Holy Scriptures," cited by Albert C. Outler, ed., *John Wesley* (New York: Oxford University Press, 1964), 123.

16. Wesley, "Preface to the Explanatory Notes upon the Old Testament," in *Works of John Wesley*, 14:252-53.

17. "Set apart a little time" ideally "every morning and evening."

18. "Read a chapter out of the Old and one out of the New Testament."

19. "A single eye" is Wesley's way of indicating a total orientation of one's being to the will of God.

20. Merton, *Opening the Bible*, 8.

21. Ibid., 20.

22. "Come Holy Ghost, Our Hearts Inspire," *The Methodist Hymnal* (Nashville: United Methodist Publishing House, 1964, 1966), hymn 131.

23. "Father of All," in John Wesley, *A Collection of Hymns for the Use of the People Called Methodists* (1780; reprint with new supplement, London: Wesleyan Conference, 1877), hymn 88.

24. "When Quiet in My House," in Wesley, *Collection of Hymns*, hymn 328.

25. Wesley, "Preface to the Sermons," in *Works of John Wesley*, 5:3.

26. Cf. Outler, *John Wesley*, 28, for his discussion on Wesley's understanding of *sola* in *sola Scriptura* being "primarily" rather than "solely."

Chapter 3

1. See, for example, Richard G. Colling, *Random Designer* (Bourbonnais, Ill.: Browning Press, 2004); Francis S. Collins, *The Language of God: A Scientist Presents Evidence for God* (Glencoe, Ill.: Free Press, 2006); Darrell R. Falk, *Coming to Peace with Science* (Downers Grove, Ill.: InterVarsity Press, 2004); John C. Polkinghorne, *Science and Providence: God's Interaction with the World* (Philadelphia: Templeton Foundation Press, 1989); Howard J. Van Till, Robert E. Snow, John H. Stek, and Davis A. Young, *Portraits of Creation: Biblical and Scientific Perspectives on the World's Formation* (Grand Rapids: William B. Eerdmans Publishing Co., 1990); Howard J. Van Till, Davis A. Young, and Clarence Menninga, *Science Held Hostage* (Downers Grove, Ill.: InterVarsity Press, 1988); Davis A. Young, *The Biblical Flood: A Case Study of the Church's Response to Extrabiblical Evidence* (Grand Rapids: William B. Eerdmans Publishing Co., 1995); and *Christianity and the Age of the Earth* (Grand Rapids: Zondervan, 1982). See also *The BioLogos Forum: Science and Faith in Dialogue*, The BioLogos Foundation, http://biologos.org/.

2. For extensive bibliographic references on Gen. 1 see Gordon J. Wenham, *Genesis 1-15*, Word Biblical Commentary (Waco, Tex.: Word Books, 1997), 1-2, and Claus Westermann, *Genesis 1-11: A Commentary*, 3 vols., trans. John J. Scullion, S.J. (Minneapolis: Augsburg Publishing House, 1974), 69-76. For the book of Genesis as a whole, see Victor P. Hamilton, *The Book of Genesis: Chapters 1-17*, The New International Commentary on the Old Testament (Grand Rapids: William B. Eerdmans Publishing Co., 1990), 75-99.

3. Daniel C. Harlow, "After Adam: Reading Genesis in an Age of Evolutionary Science," *Perspectives on Science and Christian Faith* 62, no. 3 (2010): 180.

4. For a survey of positions on inspiration by Wesleyan theologians see Robert D. Branson, "How the Discoveries of Science and Archaeology Shift Interpretations of Genesis," *Divine Grace and Emerging Creation* (Eugene, Oreg.: Pickwick Publications, 2009), 150-54.

5. Henry M. Morris, ed., *Scientific Creationism* (Green Forest, Ark.: Master Books, 1985), 204-6. Morris has written prolifically on this topic and *Scientific Creationism* represents perhaps best his position and that of other creationists. Thus this work will serve for our purposes as the primary source for this position.

6. Robert D. Branson, Jim Edlin, and Tim M. Green, *Discovering the Old Testament,* ed. Alex Varughese (Kansas City: Beacon Hill Press of Kansas City, 2003), 65.

7. Arthur McCalla, *The Creationist Debate* (New York: T. and T. Clark, 2006), 21-25.

8. Robert C. Newman and Herman J. Eckelmann Jr., *Genesis One and the Origin of the Earth* (Downers Grove, Ill.: InterVarsity Press, 1977), 69.

9. Ibid., 74.

10. Ibid., 72-73, 80.

11. Bert Thompson, *Creation Compromises* (Montgomery, Ala.: Apologetics Press, 1995), 89-103; Morris, *Scientific Creationism*, 203-4.

12. Morris, *Scientific Creationism*, 210.

13. Ibid., 211.

14. Ibid., 111.

15. Ibid., 111, 117-20.

16. Ibid., 215.

17. Ibid., 131.

18. Ibid., 137-49.

19. Young, *Christianity and the Age of the Earth*, 93-116.

20. Till et al., *Portraits of Creation*, 82-165.

21. Ibid., 267.

22. John Walton, *The Lost World of Genesis One* (Downers Grove, Ill.: InterVarsity Press, 2009). See particularly "Proposition 2," 23-37.

23. Ibid., 55-56.

24. Ibid., 56-58.

25. Ibid., 59.

26. Ibid., 66.

Chapter 4

1. The Latimer Fellowship, Orange Memorial Lecture, 1999, http://www.latimer.org.nz/downloads/woml-bible.pdf.

2. Craig Blaising, "Changing Patterns in American Dispensational Theology," *Wesleyan Theological Journal* 29, nos. 1 and 2 (Spring–Fall 1994); C. C. Ryrie, *Dispensationalism Today* (Chicago: Moody, 1965).

3. Bassett, "The Fundamentalist Leavening of the Holiness Movement: 1914-1940"; Stan Ingersol, "Strange Bedfellows: Nazarenes and Fundamentalism," *Wesleyan Theological Journal* 40, no. 2 (Fall 2005): 123-41.

4. Marsden, *Fundamentalism and American Culture*, 6, 71-101.

5. Ernest R. Sandeen, "Toward a Historical Interpretation of the Origins of Fundamentalism," *Church History* 36, no. 1 (March 1967): 66-83.

6. This is not necessarily intended as a pejorative term and does, in fact, include some learned persons trained in theology and Bible but who still cling to modes of theologizing and interpretation that are anachronistic.

7. An excellent example of this is J. I. Packer, *Fundamentalism and the Word of God* (Grand Rapids: William B. Eerdmans Publishing Co., 1958).

8. Randy Maddox, *Responsible Grace* (Nashville: Kingswood Books, 1994), 35. Cf. sermon "The Case of Reason Impartially Considered," in *Works of John Wesley*, 6:355-56.

9. Barr, *Fundamentalism*, 339.

10. George Eldon Ladd, *A Theology of the New Testament*, rev. ed. (Grand Rapids: William B. Eerdmans Publishing Co., 1993), 303.

11. John Calvin, *Institutes of the Christian Religion*, ed. Hugh T. Kerr (Philadelphia: Westminster Press, 1964), 1.8.1.

12. Paul Bassett, "Conservative Wesleyan Theology and the Challenge of Secular Humanism," *Wesleyan Theological Journal* 8 (Spring 1973): 74-75.

13. Cf. the discussion of the nature of authority in H. Ray Dunning, *Grace, Faith, and Holiness* (Kansas City: Beacon Hill Press of Kansas City, 1988), 58-62.

14. Wiley, *Christian Theology*, 1:142.

15. "The Holy Scriptures," Article IV of "Articles of Faith," *Church of the Nazarene Manual 2009-2013* (Kansas City: Nazarene Publishing House, 2009), 29.

16. N. T. Wright, "How Can the Bible Be Authoritative?" *Vox Evangelica* 21 (1991): 7-32.

17. Richard B. Hays, *The Moral Vision of the New Testament: A Contemporary Introduction to New Testament Ethics* (New York: HarperSanFrancisco, 1996), 210.

18. Ibid., 211.

19. See Mark R. Quanstrom, *A Century of Holiness Theology* (Kansas City: Beacon Hill Press of Kansas City, 2004).

Chapter 5

1. Intended as a great "Testimony to the Truth," *The Fundamentals* were published by the Bible Institute of Los Angeles between 1910 and 1915 in twelve paperback volumes. The volumes contained ninety essays.

2. See Nancy T. Ammerman's account of this conflict in "North American Protestant Fundamentalism," 2, 14.

3. Marsden, *Fundamentalism and American Culture*, 3.

4. Charles Taylor, *A Secular Age* (Boston: Belknap Press of Harvard University, 2007), 352.

5. Marsden, *Fundamentalism and American Culture*, 6.

6. Fundamentalism is often identified with millennialism (see Sandeen, *Roots of Fundamentalism*, 254-58). But the Princeton theologians were neither dispensationalists nor premillennialists. Fundamentalists such as Dwight L. Moody, Reuben A. Torrey, and C. I. Scofield embraced some form of millennialism. Millennialism is the belief that the thousand-year reign of Christ on earth mentioned in Rev. 20:4 refers to a literal period of time. Millennialism is also known as chiliasm (kee-li-asm), from the Greek word *khilioi* (thousand) and the Latin *chilias* (thousand). Millennialism in some form dates back to some of the early church fathers. Among those who interpret the text literally there is no agreement about how or when the thousand-year reign will happen. Today, the most prominent sets of answers are premillennialism, dispensational millennialism, and postmillennialism. Many scholars believe Rev. 20:1-7 should be understood symbolically or figuratively, not literally. Commenting on verse 4, John Calvin called millennialism a "fiction" and said it is "too trivial to need or to deserve refutation" (*Institutes of the Christian Religion*, 3.25.5).

Between the years 1895 and 1914 a nasty schism occurred among the millenarians over how the millennium would unfold. The dissension involved acceptance or rejection of John Nelson Darby's teaching of the "any-moment coming" of Jesus, or secret rapture. Canadian Baptist Robert Cameron charged that the Bible does not support belief in the secret rapture of Christians prior to the beginning of the millennium. The millenarians split over whether the rapture of Christians would happen before or after the tribulation. Ernest R. Sandeen details the disruption in chapter 9 of *The Roots of Fundamentalism*.

J. Gresham Machen found the term "fundamentalist" to be "distasteful" because it is pejorative. Rejecting the label, Machen said those identified as "fundamentalists" do not represent "some strange new sect." Instead, the term simply means "maintaining the historic Christian faith and of moving in the great central current of Christian life." J. Gresham Machen, *Selected Shorter Writings*, ed. D. G. Hart (Phillipsburg, N.J.: P and R Publishing, 2004), 116.

7. Charles Hodge, *Systematic Theology*, 3 vols. (Grand Rapids: William B. Eerdmans Publishing Co., 1940), a complete statement of Princeton theology.

8. J. Gresham Machen, *The Origin of Paul's Religion* (New York: Macmillan, 1921), probably Machen's best known work; *Christianity and Liberalism* (1923; reprint, Grand Rapids: William B. Eerdmans Publishing Co., 1946), a critique of liberal theology.

9. Bacon's method was based on an inductive process and was an advance over the method of Aristotle that had dominated science for centuries, but did not achieve the status of modern scientific method, which includes the use of a hypothesis. Fundamentalists opposed Darwinism as being a "hypothesis" and as not scientifically provable.

10. J. Gresham Machen, for instance, said, "The historic continuity of the Christian religion is based upon its appeal to a body of facts—facts about God and man." Machen, *Selected Shorter Writings*, 116-17.

11. Mark A. Noll, *America's God: From Jonathan Edwards to Abraham Lincoln* (New York: Oxford University Press, 2002), 93.

In chapter 6, "Theistic Common Sense," Mark Noll provides an extended examination of the influence of Scottish common sense upon the form of ethical reasoning that became almost universal in the United States in the late eighteenth century and much of the nineteenth century. The chapter's explanation of common-sense philosophy and its influence in the United States is highly recommended.

12. Ibid., 94. Noll quotes from Norman Fiering, *Jonathan Edwards's Moral Thought and Its British Context* (Chapel Hill, N.C.: University of North Carolina Press, 1981), 6-7.

13. John Witherspoon was a signer of the American Declaration of Independence. From 1776 to 1782 he was a leading member of the Continental Congress. Presbyterian minister Samuel Stanhope Smith, a student of Witherspoon and professor of moral philosophy and theology at the College of New Jersey in Princeton, "was one of America's first professional academics to study the ethics of Francis Hutcheson and also one of the first Americans to incorporate the insights of Thomas Reid into his own work" (Noll, *America's God: From Jonathan Edwards to Abraham Lincoln*, 104).

14. Reid was reacting against British empirical philosophy, represented especially by David Hume, which had proceeded on the assumption that what one knows are "ideas" in the mind, not actual objects in the external world. This had led to skepticism about any real knowledge of matters such as cause and effect, an enduring self, and God and essentially any real knowledge of the external world, all "contrary" to "common sense."

15. A major target of Scottish common-sense realism was the Scottish philosopher David Hume (1711-76). Hume rejected all claims that reason, the world, and human experience can confirm God's existence. The mind is not so constructed as to know things that transcend the empirically verifiable.

16. So said John Witherspoon, "Lectures in Divinity," *Works*, 4:28, as quoted by Noll, *America's God: From Jonathan Edwards to Abraham Lincoln*, 111.

17. Benjamin B. Warfield stated the position starkly: "There is no standing ground between . . . full verbal inspiration and no inspiration at all." Benjamin B. Warfield, *Works of Benjamin B. Warfield*, 1:173, as quoted by Fred G. Zaspel, *The Theology of B. B. Warfield: A Systematic Summary* (Wheaton, Ill.: Crossway Books, 2010), 118.

18. Hodge, *Systematic Theology*, 1:18.

19. Ammerman, "North American Protestant Fundamentalism," 9.

20. Marsden, *Fundamentalism and American Culture*, 114.

21. Sandeen, *Roots of Fundamentalism*, 118.

22. Ibid. The role of the Holy Spirit in Christian conversion was certainly not neglected. J. Gresham Machen says plainly that "the redeeming work of Christ . . . is applied to the individual soul . . . by the Holy Spirit." "Men are made Christian by the Spirit of God." Machen, *Selected Shorter Writings*, 121.

23. John Wesley, *Explanatory Notes upon the New Testament*, comment on 2 Tim. 3:16. Randy Maddox notes that "although conceptual understanding of the teaching in the Bible is vital, Wesley's deepest concern was personal *embrace* of the saving truth

in Scripture." Randy L. Maddox, "The Rule of Christian Faith, Practice, and Hope: John Wesley on the Bible," *Methodist Review* 3 (2011): 14.

24. Philip Edgcumbe Hughes, "The Reformers' View of Inspiration," *Churchman* 111, no. 4 (1997), http://www.churchsociety.org/churchman/documents/Cman_111_4_Hughes .pdf.

25. Martin Luther, "Review of Erasmus Preface," from *Bondage of the Will*, in *Martin Luther: Selections from His Writings*, ed. John Dillenberger (New York: Anchor Books, 1961), 174-75. Luther said the "perspicuity of Scripture is twofold. . . . The first is external, and relates to the ministry of the Word; the second [internal] concerns the knowledge of the heart." When speaking of the external perspicuity, "nothing whatsoever is left obscure or ambiguous, but all that is in the Scripture is through the Word brought forth into clearest light and proclaimed to the whole world" (174-75).

26. John Calvin, *Institutes of the Christian Religion*, trans. Henry Beveridge (Peabody, Mass.: Hendrickson Publishers, 2008), 1.8.1: "In vain were the authority of Scripture forti-fied by argument, or supported by the consent of the Church, or confirmed by any other helps, if unaccompanied by an assurance higher and stronger than human Judgment can give. Till this better foundation has been laid, the authority of Scripture remains in sus-pense. On the other hand, when recognizing its exemption from the common rule, we re-ceive it reverently, and according to its dignity, those proofs which were not so strong as to produce and rivet a full conviction in our minds, become most appropriate helps." The complete *Institutes* are available on line at the *Christian Classics Ethereal Library*: http://www. ccel.org/ccel/calvin/institutes.

27. Ibid., 1.7.4.

28. Ibid., 1.8.13. In his discussion of prayer, Calvin makes clear the profound limita-tions of human reason for accessing the Bible's true meaning: "The Lord kindly and spon-taneously manifests himself in Christ, in whom he offers all happiness for our misery, all abundance for our want, opening up the treasures of heaven to us, so that we may turn with full faith to his beloved Son, depend upon him with full expectation, rest in him, and cleave to him with full hope. This, indeed, is that secret and hidden philosophy which cannot be learned by syllogisms: a philosophy thoroughly understood by those whose eyes God has so opened as to see light in his light (Ps. 36:9)" (3.20.1).

29. Wesley, "Preface to the Sermons," in *Works of John Wesley*, 5:3.

30. Maddox, *Responsible Grace*, 31.

31. "This is why," says Maddox, "John Wesley never devoted significant energy to *proving* the inspiration of the Bible by appeals to its truthfulness or other such arguments" (Maddox, "Rule of Christian Faith, Practice, and Hope," 15).

32. Wesley was quoting Thomas à Kempis to Bishop William Warburton. The quote is located in Maddox, "Rule of Christian Faith, Practice, and Hope," 14.

33. William Ragsdale Cannon, *The Theology of John Wesley* (Nashville: Abingdon-Cokesbury Press, 1946), 20. Methodism

"was content merely to assert its own faith and to give testimony to the truth of God as it found that truth expressed in the Bible" (20).

34. Sandeen says, "Charles Hodge and the Princeton Theology" continually insisted that "the experiential element, the witness of the Spirit, the mystical strain, be subordinated to the matter of theological science" (Sandeen, *Roots of Fundamentalism*, 118).

35. Calvin, *Institutes of the Christian Religion*, 4.2.33.

36. Ibid., 1.8.13.

37. Hodge, *Systematic Theology*, 1:164.

38. B. B. Warfield, introduction to Francis R. Beattie's *Apologetics: Or the Rational Vindication of Christianity* (Richmond, Va.: Presbyterian Committee of Publication, 1903), in John E. Meeter, ed., *Selected Shorter Writings of Benjamin B. Warfield, II* (Nutley, N.J.: Presbyterian and Reformed Publishing Co., 1973), 103, as quoted by Marsden, *Understanding Fundamentalism and Evangelicalism*, 124.

39. Marsden, *Understanding Fundamentalism and Evangelicalism*, 135. Two important treatments of fundamentalism not referenced in this chapter are by the Scottish Old Testament scholar James Barr (1924–2006). They are *Beyond Fundamentalism: Biblical Foundations for Evangelical Christianity* (Philadelphia: Westminster Press, 1984); and *Fundamentalism* (Harrisburg, Pa.: Trinity Press International, 1981).

40. Marsden, *Understanding Fundamentalism and Evangelicalism*, 135.

41. Ibid., 136-37.

42. Charles Darwin, "Chapter 14—Recapitulation and Conclusion," *The Origin of Species* (1859), Literature.org, http://www.literature.org/authors/darwin-charles/the-origin-of-species/chapter-14.html.

43. When the new science of population genetics was wedded to Darwin's theory of natural selection, Darwinism became Neo-Darwinism.

44. Historian of American Christianity Sydney E. Ahlstrom says, "The Scottish Philosophy is no longer in good repute despite its proud reign in another day. Indeed, few, if any, schools of philosophy have been given such disdainful treatment by historians as Common Sense Realism." Ahlstrom asks, "Was the Scottish philosophy as undistinguished as posterity has judged it to be?" He answers the question with a "qualified negative" (Sydney E. Ahlstrom, "The Scottish Philosophy and American Theology," *Church History* 24, no. 3 (September 1955): 257-72.

45. Darwin, "Chapter 14—Recapitulation and Conclusion."

46. William Placher, *The Triune God: An Essay in Postliberal Theology* (Louisville, Ky.: Westminster John Knox Press, 2007), 10.

47. Ibid., 21.

Chapter 6

1. An overview of the extensive "science and religion" dialog can be found in Ian Barbour, *When Science Meets Religion: Enemies,*

Strangers, or Partners? (New York: HarperCollins, 2000) or John Polkinghorne, *Science and Theology: An Introduction* (Minneapolis: Fortress Press, 1998).

2. Maddox, *Responsible Grace.*

3. Randy L. Maddox, "John Wesley's Precedent for Theological Engagement with the Natural Sciences," *Wesleyan Theological Journal* 44, no. 1 (Spring 2009): 23-54.

4. Ibid., 34.

5. Paul Copan and William Lane Craig, *Creation out of Nothing: A Biblical, Philosophical, and Scientific Exploration* (Grand Rapids: Baker Academic, 2004).

6. Additional examples include "Einstein rings," which are caused by the gravitational bending of light from distant galaxies. Some pictures can be found by searching for "Einstein Ring" on the Hubble Telescope website, hubblesite.org.

7. For example, the Global Positioning System (GPS) relies on precise clocks aboard satellites orbiting earth. These clocks must be corrected for the time-warping effects of general (and special) relativity. If they were not, the GPS system would accumulate error at the rate of about six miles per day.

8. Einstein's relativity predicted this expansion of space, but he was so certain space in the universe was static that he added a cancelling "fudge factor" into his equations in what he would later call the biggest blunder of his career. (It actually turns out that this correction is needed but for a different reason.)

9. Penzias and Wilson actually accidentally "scooped" another group that was actively looking for this signal, and they eventually won a Nobel Prize for their discovery.

10. For information about the WMAP satellite, visit the NASA mission website: http://map.gsfc.nasa.gov/.

11. The spectrum of the CMB perfectly matches a theoretical "black body" spectrum that would be produced by a hot object such as the glowing-hot element of an electric stove.

12. Augustine, *Confessions* (New York: Penguin Books, 1961), 11.13.

13. For a more comprehensive treatment of the science behind this argument, see Paul Davies, *The Goldilocks Enigma: Why Is the Universe Just Right for Life?* (New York: Mariner Books, 2008).

14. For a treatment of fine-tuning from a theological perspective, see Alister McGrath, *A Fine-Tuned Universe: The Quest for God in Science and Theology* (Louisville, Ky.: Westminster John Knox Press, 2009).

15. For example, some scientists argue for an almost infinite number of universes with different physical laws, and of course we exist in one of the universes that support life (anthropic selection in a multiverse). This does not solve the ultimate problem, however, because we then must ask where all of those universes came from.

16. In addition to quantum uncertainty, many systems in nature exhibit an extreme sensitivity to initial conditions (chaos) that would amplify quantum effects that would normally be seen only on a small scale.

17. See for example, Ted Peters and Martinez Hewlett, *Can You Believe in God and Evolution? A Guide for the Perplexed*

(Nashville: Abington, 2006) or John Polkinghorne and Nicholas Beale, *Questions of Truth: Fifty-one Responses to Questions About God, Science, and Belief* (Louisville, Ky.: Westminster John Knox Press, 2009), 138.

18. Francis Collins, *The Language of God: A Scientist Presents Evidence for Belief* (Glencoe, Ill.: Free Press, 2007), 141.

19. For example, even modern science has recognized that organisms are more than just the sum of their DNA. An Internet search for "Systems Biology" will highlight the increasingly more holistic approach to biology.

20. Charles Wesley, "Jesus, Thine All Victorious Love," Cyber Hymnal, http://www .hymntime.com/tch/htm/j/t/a/jtavlove.htm.

21. Collins, *Language of God*, 109-43.

22. The deactivated GLO sequence does have differences in current primates, but this is expected since mutations in the nonfunctional gene can be passed down without causing negative effects. Also, some intermediate sequences (those that don't code for proteins) do have important functions, but there are demonstrated examples that pseudogenes can be deleted from an organism's genome without any negative effects.

23. Maddox writes that Wesley "repeatedly argued that if humans had not been *graced* with liberty, they would not have been capable of either virtue or guilt, that is, they could not have been *responsible*" (Maddox, *Responsible Grace*, 70).

24. Karl Giberson and Francis Collins, *The Language of Science and Faith* (Downers Grove, Ill.: InterVarsity Press, 2011), 50.

25. If we affirm that we are granted freedom by God (free will), and we know that we are part of nature, then it should not be surprising that God grants a degree of freedom to nature itself. Without any freedom in nature, we as natural creatures could not have free will.

26. These arguments usually assume that if a natural explanation can be found, God was not involved. This is why we should be careful not to fill in the gaps in our scientific understanding with special "supernatural" acts of God. God is always supernatural (above nature) even while continually working in and through nature.

27. Jürgen Moltmann, *Sun of Righteousness, Arise! God's Future for Humanity and the World* (Philadelphia: Fortress Press, 2010), 67.

28. Jürgen Moltmann, *Experiences in Theology* (Philadelphia: Augsburg Fortress Publishers, 2000), 337.

Chapter 7

1. Wesley, "Of the Church," in *Works of John Wesley*, 6:395-96.

2. "The Church" Article XI of "Articles of Faith," *Church of the Nazarene Manual 2009-2013*, 34-35.

3. Ibid.

4. "The General Church," Article I of "The Church," *Church of the Nazarene Manual 2009-2013*, 37.

5. "The Churches Severally," Article II of "The Church," *Church of the Nazarene Manual 2009-2013*, 37.

6. "Agreed Statement of Belief," Article IV of "The Church," *Church of the Nazarene Manual 2009-2013*, 37.

7. Ibid., 37-38.

8. Wesley, "A Caution Against Bigotry," in *Works of John Wesley*, 5:490.

9. Ibid., 484-85.

10. "The Covenant of Christian Character," Article V of "The Church," *Church of the Nazarene Manual 2009-2013*, 38-40.

11. Ibid.

12. Preamble to "Government," Part IV of *Church of the Nazarene Manual 2009-2013*, 62.

13. Ibid.

14. Wesley, "On Schism," in *Works of John Wesley*, 2:401-10.

15. For some current topics that require discussion, see Daniel Boone, *A Charitable Discourse: Talking About the Things That Divide Us* (Kansas City: Beacon Hill Press of Kansas City, 2011).

Chapter 8

1. See Joel B. *Green, Seized by Truth: Reading the Bible as Scripture* (Nashville: Abingdon, 2007); J. Todd Billings, *The Word of God for the People of God: An Entryway to the Theological Interpretation of Scripture* (Grand Rapids: Eerdmans, 2007); Daniel J. Treier, *Introducing Theological Interpretation of Scripture: Recovering a Christian Practice* (Grand Rapids: Baker Academic, 2008).

2. "Religion Among the Millennials," February 17, 2010, Pew Forum on Religion and Public Life, http://pewforum.org/Age/Religion-Among-the-Millennials.aspx (accessed February 21, 2011); *The Gallup Poll: Public Opinion 2007* (Lanham, Md.: Rowman and Littlefield, 2008), 229.

3. I have taken these definitions from J. I. Packer, "Infallibility and Inerrancy of the Bible," in *New Dictionary of Theology*, ed. Sinclair B. Ferguson and David F. Wright (Downers Grove, Ill.: InterVarsity, 1988), 337-39.

4. Joel B. Green, *Reading Scripture As Wesleyans* (Nashville: Abingdon Press, 2010), i-viii.

5. Wesley, "The Character of a Methodist," in *Works of John Wesley*, 8:340.

6. Ibid., 341.

7. Ibid.

8. Wesley, "The Way to the Kingdom," in *Works of John Wesley*, 5:78.

9. Wesley, "Preface to the Sermons," in *Works of John Wesley*, 5:3.